THE STANDARDBREDS

THE STANDARDBREDS

by Barbara J. Berry

SOUTH BRUNSWICK AND NEW YORK: A. S. BARNES AND COMPANY
LONDON: THOMAS YOSELOFF LTD

A. S. Barnes and Co., Inc.
Cranbury, New Jersey 08512

Thomas Yoseloff Ltd
Magdalen House
136–148 Tooley Street
London SE1 2TT, England

Library of Congress Cataloging in Publication Data

Berry, Barbara J
   The standardbreds.

   Bibliography: p.
   1. Standardbred horse. 2. Harness racehorses. 3. Harness racing. I. Title.
SF293.S72B47   636.1'7   78-69690
ISBN 0-498-02251-X

To the "Number One Crew"
of the Frenchman

Contents

Acknowledgments

The author is most grateful to Donald Evans, Vice President of Publicity and Public Relations of The United States Trotting Association and to S. Rhoads of the photo department of the USTA, for providing the fine illustrations.

How the Old Horse Won the Bet

The following poem has long been a favorite of mine, and you, too, may enjoy this masterful description of an old-time, "under saddle" trotting race, with its surprise ending.

How the Old Horse Won the Bet
by Oliver Wendell Holmes

'Twas on the famous trotting-ground,
The betting men were gathered round
From far and near; the "cracks" were there
Whose deeds the sporting prints declare:
The swift g.m., Old Hiram's nag,
The fleet s.h., Dan Pfeiffer's brag,
With these a third — and who is he
That stands beside his fast b.g.?
Budd Doble, whose catarrhal name
So fills the nasal trump of fame.
There too stood many a noted steed
Of Messenger and Morgan breed;
Green horses, also, not a few;
Unknown as yet what they could do:
And all the hacks that know so well
The scourgings of the Sunday swell.

Blue are the skies of opening day;
The bordering turf is green with May;
The sunshine's golden gleam is thrown
On sorrel, chestnut, bay and roan;
The horses paw and prance and neigh,
Fillies and colts like kittens play,
And dance and toss their rippled manes
Shining and soft as silken skeins;
Wagons and gigs are ranged about,
And fashion flaunts her gay turn-out;
Here stands — each youthful Jehu's dream —
The jointed tandem, ticklish team!
And there in ampler breadth expand
The splendors of the four-in-hand;

On faultless ties and glossy tiles
The lovely bonnets beam their smiles;

11

(The style's the man, so books avow;
The style's the woman, anyhow);
From flounces frothed with creamy lace
Peeps out the pug-dog's smutty face,
Or spaniel rolls his liquid eye,
Or stares the wiry pet of Skye,—
O woman, in your hours of ease
So shy with us, so free with these!

"Come on! I'll bet you two to one
I'll make him do it!" "Will you? Done!"

What was it who was bound to do?
I did not hear and can't tell you,—
Pray listen till my story's through.

Scarce noticed, back behind the rest,
By cart and wagon rudely prest,
The parson's lean and bony bay
Stood harnessed in his one-horse shay—
Lent to his sexton for the day
(A funeral,—so the sexton said;
His mother's uncle's wife was dead).

Like Lazarus bid to Dive's feast,
So looked the poor forlorn old beast;
His coat was rough, his tail was bare,
The gray was sprinkled in his hair;
Sportsmen and jockeys knew him not,
And yet they say he once could trot
Among the fleetest of the town,
Till something cracked and broke him down,—
The steed's the statesman's, common lot!
"And are we then so soon forgot?"
Ah, me! I doubt if one of you
Has ever heard the name "Old Blue,"
Whose fame through all this region rung
In those old days when I was young!

"Bring forth the horse!" Alas! he showed
Not like the one Mazeppa rode;
Scant-maned, sharp-backed, and shaky-kneed,
The wreck of what was once a steed,
Lips thin, eyes hollow, stiff in joints;
Yet not without his knowing points.
The sexton laughing in his sleeve,
As if 't were all a make-believe,
Led forth the horse, and as he laughed,
Unhitched the breeching from a shaft,

Unclasped the rusty belt beneath,
Drew forth the snaffle from his teeth,
Slipped off his head-stall, set him free
From strap and rein,— a sight to see!

So worn, so lean in every limb,
It can't be they are saddling him!
It is! His back the pig-skin strides
And flaps his lank, rheumatic sides;
With look of mingled scorn and mirth
They buckle round the saddle-girth;
With horsy wink and saucy toss
A youngster throws his leg across,
And so, his rider on his back,
They lead him, limping, to the track,
Far up behind the starting point,
To limber out each stiffened joint.

As through the jeering crowd he past,
One pitying look Old Hiram cast;
"Go it, ye cripple, while ye can!"
Cried out unsentimental Dan;
"A Fast-day dinner for the crows!"
Budd Doble's scoffing shout arose.

Slowly, as when the walking-beam
First feels the gathering head of steam,
With warning cough and threatening wheeze
The stiff old charger crooks his knees;
At first with cautious step sedate,
As if he dragged a coach of state;
He's not a colt; he knows full well
That time is weight and sure to tell;
No horse so sturdy but he fears
The handicap of twenty years.

As through the throng on either hand
The old horse nears the judges' stand;
Beneath his jockey's feather-weight
He warms a little to his gait,
And now and then a step is tried
That hints of something like a stride.

"Go!"—Through his ear the summons stung
As if a battle-trump had rung;
The slumbering instincts long unstirred
Start at the old familiar word;
It thrills like flame through every limb,—
What mean his twenty years to him?

The savage blow his rider dealt
Fell on his hollow flanks unfelt;
The spur that pricked his staring hide
Unheeded tore his bleeding side;
Alike to him are spur and rein,—
He steps a five-year-old again!

Before the quarter pole was past,
Old Hiram said, "He's going fast."
Long ere the quarter was a half,
The chuckling crowd had ceased to laugh;
Tighter his frightened jockey clung
As in a mighty stride he swung,
The gravel flying in his track,
His neck stretched out, his ears laid back,
His tail extended all the while
Behind him like a rat-tail file!
Off went a shoe,—away it spun,
Shot like a bullet from a gun;
The quaking jockey shapes a prayer
From scraps of oaths he used to swear;
He drops his whip, he drops his rein,
He clutches fiercely for a mane;
He'll lose his hold—he sways and reels—
He'll slide beneath those trampling heels!
The knees of many a horseman quake,
The flowers on many a bonnet shake,
And shouts arise from left and right,
"Stick on! Stick on!"   "Hould tight!   Hould tight!"
"Cling round his neck and don't let go—
That pace can't hold—there!   steady!   whoa!"
But like the sable steed that bore
The spectral lover of Lenore,
His nostrils snorting foam and fire,
No stretch his bony limbs can tire;
And now the stand he rushes by,
And "Stop him!—stop him!" is the cry,
Stand back! he's only just begun—
He's having out three heats in one!

"Don't rush in front! he'll smash your brains;
But follow up and grab the reins!"
Old Hiram spoke, Dan Pfeiffer heard,
And sprang impatient at the word;
Budd Doble started on his bay,
Old Hiram followed on his gray,
And off they spring, and round they go,
The fast ones doing "all they know."
Look! Twice they follow at his heels,

As round the circling course he wheels,
And whirls with him that clinging boy
Like Hector round the walls of Troy;
Still on, and on, the third time round!
They're tailing off! they're losing ground!
Budd Doble's nag begins to fail!
Dan Pfeiffer's sorrel whisks his tail!
And see! in spite of whip and shout,
Old Hiram's mare is giving out!
Now for the finish! at the turn,
The old horse — all the rest astern —
Comes swinging in, with easy trot;
By Jove! he's distanced all the lot!

That trot no mortal could explain;
Some said, "Old Dutchman come again!"
Some took his time, — at least they tried,
But what it was none could decide;
One said he couldn't understand
What happened to his second hand;
One said 2:10; *that* couldn't be —
More like two twenty-two or -three;
Old Hiram settled it at last;
"The time was two — too dee-vel-ish fast!"

The parson's horse had won the bet;
It cost him something of a sweat;
Back in the one-horse shay he went;
The parson wondered what it meant,
And murmured, with a mild surprise,
And pleasant twinkle of the eyes,
"That funeral must have been a trick,
Or corpses drive at double-quick;
I shouldn't wonder, I declare,
If brother — Jehu — made the prayer!"

And this is all I have to say
About that tough old trotting bay.
Huddup! Huddup!   G'lang!   Good day!

Moral for which this tale is told:
A horse *can* trot, for all he's old.

THE STANDARDBREDS

1
THE STANDARDBRED

The Standardbred is, indisputably and by far, the fastest trotting and pacing horse in the world. It is also, unlike its second cousin the Thoroughbred, a completely American development. And for the most part this new American breed was created from England's "scraps"—horses that the mother country considered too inferior to keep. So it also represents a monumental triumph of "Yankee ingenuity."

There are, of course, other wonderful breeds that were first developed in America from much the same "scraps"—the Morgan, the American Saddle Horse, the Tennessee Walking Horse and the Quarter Horse come to mind— but of them all, only the Standardbred has achieved truly world-wide fame. There are other countries with fast trotters and pacers, but wherever there are *extremely* fast trotters and pacers there are horses whose pedigrees are heavy with imported Standardbred blood. There is simply no other breed of horse on earth that can compare with the Standardbred in this respect.

The Thoroughbred and the Standardbred are, in fact, probably more well-known in more countries than any other breed except the Arabian. And they are both "specialists"; primarily, they are superlative race horses. Although there are considerably more Thoroughbreds in the world today than there are Standardbreds, this may not hold true indefinitely. The Standardbred's sport, harness racing, is mushrooming in popularity, and in this country at least, it is actually overtaking Thoroughbred racing. With harness tracks highly successful and proliferating, and harness race purses soaring ever skyward, the potential is limitless. Fads and fashions being what they are, however, time alone will tell.

The Standardbred breeder finds himself at somewhat of a disadvantage in one respect. Even the best breeding farms do not produce good race horses from each and every mating, and the Thoroughbred breeder can quite easily sell his "almost-rans" as riding horses, especially as hunters and jumpers. But the Standardbred, while it can certainly be ridden, is not a popular riding horse, because neither of its two best gaits is particularly comfortable.

19

Nevele Pride is a fine example of the modern-day Standardbred.

Therefore, the value of a non-raceworthy Thoroughbred is generally considerably higher than that of its trotting and/or pacing equivalent. This difference doesn't mean much to the large, successful breeding establishments, but to the many smaller breeders it can mean a great deal.

At one time this situation was vastly different. A well-bred road horse was worth almost as much as a winning race horse, and the demand at times actually exceeded the supply. But then Henry Ford's "consarned contraption" revolutionized transportation throughout the country, and in an amazingly short period of time a good road horse was absolutely worthless. Harness racing itself took a hard blow from the arrival of the automobile, too. It suffered a near collapse that lasted for several years, until strong measures were taken by strong men, and the condition we see today — a glowingly healthy sport — is the fortunate result.

Today's Standardbred, as might be expected, comes closer to being a uniform type than it has ever been before. There are still frequent atypical

Steve Lobell, driven by W. Haughton, clearly demonstrates the trotter's diagonal gait.

specimens, as there are in most breeds, but generally speaking the modern Standardbred stands between 15 and 16 hands high, runs to solid colors (with nearly half of them being bay), and is of a distinctly "racey" appearance. Quite often this is enhanced by the typical "trotting pitch"—the slightly higher hips that produce a downward-toward-the-front slope which gives the impression of speed even when the horse is at rest. The average Standardbred is not really a "beautiful" animal in the show horse sense. It is more apt to be, in fact, quite ordinary and sometimes even somewhat coarse-appearing, with a plain head, straight neck, large ears, and angular form. The Standardbred's own kind of beauty is there, however, to those who know him well, in his intelligent tractability, his tremendous courage and endless willingness to "do," and, of course, in his devastating speed.

The Standardbred's most outstanding trait is this great speed at the trot or at the pace. Some Standardbreds can even perform about equally well at both gaits. There has been a great deal of argument among breeding theorists ever since the breed began as to which gait is dominant, or "the true gait," and which is merely an offshoot or a "poor relation." The trot is natural to most horses, a gait in which the two legs on diagonally opposite "corners" move in unison, which is why it is called a diagonal gait. This causes a springy motion, and the horse's back rises and falls noticeably. The pace, on the other hand, is a lateral gait, wherein the pair of legs on each *side* move together. This does not result in much up-and-down movement, but produces rather more of a side-to-side swaying effect. The pace, unlike the trot, is not natural to most kinds of horses.

But it is important to remember that while most horses can trot naturally, it is also natural to them to break into a canter or gallop at anything above a moderate speed. Therefore it is a definite, distinct breed characteristic of the Standardbred that allows it to trot (or pace) at a great rate of speed without offering to break gait. This is what distinguishes it from the "running horse," or Thoroughbred, and from the saddle breeds in general.

John H. Wallace, an eminent authority and the man most responsible for establishing a breed registry for "the American Standard Trotting-Bred Horse," was of the firm opinion that "speed at the trot comes from speed at the pace." He felt that the two gaits were really one, pacing blood being the essential without which speed at either gait could not be bred. John Hervey, however, perhaps equally knowledgeable and writing fifty years later than Wallace, in 1946, disagreed heartily. To him, pacers were "inferior" and not much more than a nuisance to the breed. It is almost a question of which came first, the chicken or the egg.

The fact remains that although the breed is registered in the Trotting Register, is administered by the United States Trotting Association, and is proud of its Hall of Fame of the Trotter, the vast majority of the Standardbreds

The lateral gait of the pacer is often encouraged and controlled by pacing hobbles, once called "Indiana pants."

John H. Wallace, author of The Horse of America, *established the first registry for the "American Standard Trotting-Bred Horse."*

John L. Hervey, author of The American Trotter, *often disagreed with Wallace's opinions, especially about the influence of pacing blood in the breed.*

now in action are pacers. This seems highly paradoxical, but we'll be seeing later how that happened.

To find out how such a remarkable new breed came about, it has been necessary to search through numerous books, some of them quite old. I have taken the liberty of quoting at length from some of these, because they are no longer readily available to the casual reader. Being valuable, they are in fact often hidden away in reference sections where they must be ordered up, and so I have "recycled" parts of them here in the hope of recapturing for you some of the unique flavor of the times in which they were written, and in order that they not be lost and forgotten altogether.

In the process, I have been brought to the inescapable conclusion that while the development of the Standardbred was an extremely logical, almost inevitable evolution, it was most assuredly "no accident." In only about fifty years our astute American horsemen produced a far superior type of horse to any of the "scraps" they originally had to work with, a type that bred on so reliably as to become a true breed. Moreover, it was a breed which, when exported to England and Europe, completely, absolutely, and humiliatingly wiped out all competition, including the Russian Czar's famed Orloff Trotters.

But, as they say, they did it "with a little bit of luck." For it was certainly a lucky day when, for instance, England decided it no longer wanted Messenger. And it was another lucky day when English horsemen learned to post to the trot, because on that day they cast aside their plain little pacers and shipped many of them off to the colonies in the New World, where the people wouldn't realize they were "unfashionable." That, really, was the beginning of the Standardbred.

2
THE PACERS

Prior to about 1600, the favorite riding horses in England were the Irish Hobbies and the Scottish Galloways. Both these types evidently descended from horses brought to Great Britain by first the Phoenicians and later on the Romans, many years before Christ. Both types were also well known for their preference for the pacing gait, although they seem to have been either very versatile individuals or else not of a very uniform type, since both Hobbies and Galloways were famed as running racehorses, as well as pacers and trotters. And they were both small, little (if any) over 13 hands, or what today would be considered pony-sized.

The little Hobbies and "pacing Galloways" were highly valued as "easy-gaited saddlers." Now, this seems extremely odd to us, especially to those of us who have ever ridden a pacing horse. The slight but noticeable sideways swaying, with the "bump in the middle," far from seeming easy-gaited can bring on a state closely resembling seasickness. At least that's been my own experience. So a suspicion arose when I read this over and over, and upon further searching I found a clue that bolstered this suspicion in a book written in 1866 by Hiram Woodruff, the renowned trainer-driver of the most successful, very earliest, trotting race horses.

In discussing some of the famous trotters of the day that had once paced (at that time pacers were looked down upon and never raced), Mr. Woodruff commented: "Another very remarkable instance was that of Cayuga Chief. This horse was not only a pacer, but single-footed when at a moderate rate, like the old Narragansett pacers . . . He paced fast when called upon; but, carrying a lady, he always went ambling off single-footed, in the easiest and most gentle style."

This makes rather more sense. "Ambling," or single-footing, is about the smoothest, most comfortable ride there is. It also makes it a lot easier to see how our "saddle-gaited" horse, the American Saddle Horse, and the Tennessee Walker with its smooth, gliding, "running walk," developed these gaits from so much pacing blood. It helps to remember that those early, "easy-gaited pacers" *also* single-footed. From this and other clues found, then, I think it is safe to assume from now on when we read about easy-gaited pacers that they were also amblers.

Neither pacing nor ambling was probably a truly natural gait, but both had been encouraged by training and selective breeding from ancient times until they became "natural" in certain strains, like the Hobbies and Galloways of Great Britain. John H. Wallace went to great trouble to prove, however, that the pacing gait was natural, as well as of ancient origin, by pointing to surviving monuments and carvings of pacing horses. He also quoted John Lawrence, a highly-respected horseman who wrote in 1800:

"That natural and most excellent pace, the trot, seems to have been very little prized or attended to by the ancients, and was, indeed, by the Romans held in a kind of contempt, or aversion, as is demonstrated by the terms which served to describe it. A trotting horse was called by them *successator*, or shaker, and sometimes, *cruciator*, or tormentor . . ."

I might interject here, to avoid too much confusion, that the above use of the word "pace" is in its meaning as "gait," as in "to put him through his paces."

Mr. Wallace then went on to prove that there were indeed pacers in early England, by quoting Fitz Stephen, a Canterbury monk who died in 1191:

> There is without one of the gates, immediately in the suburb [of London], a certain smooth field (Smithfield) in name and reality. There every Friday, unless it be one of the more solemn festivals, is a noted show of well-bred horses exposed for sale. The earls, barons and knights . . . as well as most of the citizens, flock thither either to look or to buy. It is pleasant to see the nags with their sleek and shining coats, smoothly ambling (pacing) along, raising and setting down, as it were, their feet on either side; in one part (of the field) are horses better adapted to the esquires; those whose pace is rougher, yet expeditious, lift up and set down, as it were, the two apposite fore and hind feet (trotting) together.

Apparently all the parenthetical terms in this were inserted by Wallace, to help prove his point that there were natural pacers in England before 1191. In fact, however, Fitz Stephen did say "amble" and *not* "pace," as Wallace interpreted it in his parentheses. The good monk's subsequent description of the gait he meant does sound like a pace (as it were) but it has been my own observation that many of the single-footing or ambling gaits, including that known as the "broken pace," could be so described, especially by a non-horseman. Throughout history the very words used to describe various gaits have changed several times, and even today, for that matter, a person would be hard put to accurately *describe* some of the single-footing gaits and the subtle differences among them, so similar are they.

Therefore, it is just possible that Fitz Stephen meant exactly what he said when he used the word "amble," rather than Wallace's "pace," and it is certainly true that the pure pace and the various single-footing or ambling gaits are very closely related. It is also certain that horses with a strong tendency toward these closely-related gaits were common in England until the end of the 1600s.

Even Mr. Hervey agreed with that. He seemed to object to Wallace's insistence that this pacing gait (or whatever) was *natural* to them, and he objected even more strongly to Wallace's "obsession" that pacing blood is elemental to and necessary in, the "trotting-bred horse." His own stand was that pacing blood should be kept right out of the trotter's breeding and that it is in fact detrimental to it.

Referring to those same surviving monuments, carvings and bits of writing from ancient times, Hervey points out a fact that Wallace seemed to prefer to gloss over — that they also show that much training went into producing those comfortable, non-trotting gaits, by the widespread use of hobbles, rollers, weights, and other equipment still in use today for much the same purpose. He further pointed out that the name Hobbie was derived from the word "hobble."

Both men seem to agree, though, that one way or another the "pacing" horse was highly valued, hence cultivated and encouraged, throughout Europe and in England for something like a thousand years, while the trotting horse was neglected and even discouraged. This is quite understandable when we remember that all this time the most common means of travel was by horseback, not by drawn vehicles, and that even the pure pace, let alone the wonderfully comfortable single-footing gaits, is eminently preferable on a long journey to the bone-rattling trot of the "tormentor."

Where Hervey and Wallace part ways again is in Wallace's continued assertion (and he could be extremely assertive!) that this pacing blood was all-important, and that fast trotters were merely more or less a fortunate offshoot of it. Meanwhile Hervey just as firmly contended that trotting, being the more natural of the two gaits, had only slipped into disuse through a millenium of neglect and had but to *overcome* the (to him) unfortunate pacing tendencies — by then inherent in the strains, to achieve extreme speed at the trot.

Whatever the truth may be in all of this fascinating discussion, the England of the early 1600s brought to fruition three important factors that would with comparative suddenness bring the trotter back into style, and consequently bring the "easy-gaited pacer" that had served so well for so long into such disfavor that it totally disappeared from the British Isles. In less than a hundred years, in fact, the pacer was actually forgotten.

The first of these factors was that England finally began to get some halfway decent roads, and began to learn how to maintain them so that they were passable throughout much of the year. Coaches became safer to ride in, although they still had a disconcerting way of tipping over in deep ruts, and they could be more dependably scheduled. And private vehicles became much more common and widespread as soon as there were roads adequate to accommodate them, where before carriages had been pretty much limited to city driving and dry weather. In short, the common mode of "getting there" changed from afoot-and-horseback to four-wheel drive.

This shift in the common means of transportation was accompanied by a shift in the typé of horses most in demand. For riding, the honest little pacer could not be beaten. But for coaches, carriages, and buggies, larger, more stylish horses were preferred, and it was soon seen that the pacer's low, smooth, rapid but definitely not dashing gait was nowhere near as stylish as a big trot. The pacer simply became unfashionable.

The second factor in the growing disfavor of the homely little pacer seems insignificant at first glance but may be the most important of all. The British, with their new, high-stepping, bold-trotting carriage horses, liked to "put on the dog" a little by adding postillions to their equippage. These fellows rode atop the carriage horses, all dressed in fine livery, and helped to manage them, although their primary purpose seems to have been in adding status to the whole rig-out. And these big, fine-looking horses were an entirely different matter to ride than the easy little pacers. In sheer self-defense, the postillions were soon forced to learn the knack of rising to the trot—that is, landing upon the horse's back only at every other stride.

Their fellow countrymen probably, on noticing this strange new way of riding, ridiculed it. But the pacer going out of style even for riding, and trotting being so much more impressive-looking, they too soon learned to "post" to the trot. And so it wasn't long before even England's saddle stock was larger, flashier, and strictly three-gaited. They walked, trotted and cantered. The pacer was no longer needed, for either saddle or harness.

To obtain this new saddle stock, as well as to furnish the (now-required) coach and carriage horses, some Hobbie and Galloway blood was of necessity used, particularly in Norfolk County where there was developed the "ideal coach horse," the Norfolk trotter. Still small by modern standards, the Norfolk trotted more often than he paced or galloped, had plenty of style and more than enough speed, and was soon in much demand, especially when the new-fangled railroads began to threaten the coaching business. We must try to keep this Norfolk breed in mind, because it was extremely important, with its trotting propensity, in forming the Standardbred. Its blood was also present in the Thoroughbred's origins, although it was not exactly welcome there.

The third factor that contributed to the banishment and indeed the deliberate breeding-out of the pacer in England in the 1600s was the advent of the "Oriental" horses. Not much larger than the Hobbies and Galloways, they had some advantages. They were "new" and all the rage; they were beautiful, which the pacers were not; and, most importantly they were avidly taken up by royalty and by the royalty-emulating aristocracy. Moreover, in spite of the fact that the diminutive Hobbies and Galloways out-raced them at the gallop so disastrously that the glamourous Orientals (Barbs, Turks and Arabians) were habitually given a considerable weight advantage, it was the fashionable Oriental stallions that were being used upon the native-bred mares to create the new "English blood horse" that would one day be called the Thoroughbred.

Then, as now and always, England had little sustained interest in organized trotting or pacing races. The running race was literally the sport of kings and as such set the style for the country. England had right at hand all the ingredients for the Standardbred, but she did not develop it. Instead, she shipped the ingredients to the colonies, which supplied the recipe and stirred it well. England was almost forced to use some of its pacing blood in the creation of its Thoroughbred, but it was never proud of the fact and even tried to hide it behind false pedigrees. A good example is the "pedigree" of the famed running race horse Bald Galloway, foaled in 1708 and one of the last of his kind. He was the sire of the famous mare Roxana, who when bred to the Godolphin Arabian produced Cade, the sire of Matchem, one of the three "pillars of the (Thoroughbred) Stud Book." A plain, old-fashioned "pacing Galloway," not deemed suitable as an ancestor for such an exalted stallion as Matchem, he was duly furnished with a pedigree "all of foreign blood and ending in a "Royal Mare." This kind of pedigree fiddling was not too uncommon at that time, and indicates all too clearly the status of the pacer by then.

But, just as the pacer was about to be wiped out of existence, at least in Britain, there were colonies being settled in the New World. Here were colonies that, of course, had no roads whatsoever, let alone good ones, and colonists who, being out of touch with the latest fads in the mother country (and being eminently practical besides), saw nothing wrong at all with "easy-gaited pacers," and welcomed them. It was an ideal arrangement that allowed England to get rid of the horses it no longer wanted or needed, at the same time providing the colonies with just exactly what they wanted and needed. It is interesting to consider that if the American colonies had been founded and settled a hundred years later than they were, by which time the pacer had virtually disappeared in England, the Standardbred would probably not exist today.

3

THE FIRST AMERICAN BREED

The Puritans arrived at Plymouth Rock in 1620, and Salem was settled not long after. For nine years these Massachusetts colonies managed to get along without any horses whatever. Then in 1629 the Salem congregation's minister, Francis Higginson, imported about half a dozen horses from England. This started the ball rolling and immediately the London Company began to include a few horses in its subsequent shipments to Salem. The Plymouth Colony apparently didn't get the idea until 1632, when it too began to import horses. Horses became more necessary, naturally, as the settlements took hold and began to spread out, and as larger fields were cleared and planted.

Meanwhile the Virginians, having been in Jamestown since 1607 and (being "cavaliers") having brought horses with them, were a little ahead of the New Englanders. Not by much, however. For one thing, due to a hard winter and famine their first year, the Virginians had been forced to use those first horses as groceries. They were not shy about asking for replacements, though, and imported more horses regularly until they had "increased and multiplied," so much that in 1669 a law was passed prohibiting further importations.

The Dutch actually arrived here before the English, of course, following Henry Hudson's discovery of New York harbor and the river he first hoped was a way to the Orient. But the first Dutch "settlers" were little more than fur traders, the Dutch being traders above all else, until 1625 when a more permanent type of settler arrived in "Newe Amsterdam." Like the Virginians, these Dutch brought horses along with them.

And long before any of this, Columbus had returned to the West Indies, bringing and leaving horses there, and during the 1500s quite a few Spanish-type horses arrived on those islands.

So there were soon three basic types of horses in the New World—the small, general-utility and easy-gaited English pacing horse; the larger, heavier (but still tiny by present-day reckoning) Dutch horse; and the Spanish, Barb-type horse. That the English and Dutch horses were eventually interbred has been well established. Just what, if any, effect the Spanish horses had upon the "American" horse is doubtful. About 1643, a shipload of them was brought up to New Amsterdam but they seem not to have acclimated themselves well and the few that survived were four years later sold off to the Virginians. Some historians claim that these Spanish horses ambled. Although Wallace denies such a probability, if amblers had been common throughout Europe for a thousand years, it seems likely enough that these could have been amblers, too. The further claim by a few that this brief contact with Spanish blood was responsible for the subsequent pacing tendencies in the Northern stock, however, seems far-fetched.

For what were those English horses that were imported constantly into New England and Virginia from about 1620 onward? They were pacers—amblers. Little Hobbies and Galloways, the "rejects" of the mother country. If the bit of Spanish blood that might have got into the developing American road horse had any real effect at all along those lines, it was certainly not an essential one.

The home of The United States Trotting Association in Columbus, Ohio.

But what were the Dutch horses? We know that they were larger, heavier, and brought higher prices than the English imports. We also know that Holland at that time had more than one kind of horse. These were definitely not of the huge Flanders draft type; they didn't measure over 14 hands high and they were, as soon as England won over New Amsterdam in 1664, used as running race horses, so they couldn't have been *too* ponderous.

Wallace delved long and deeply into this mystery, coming up with the conclusion that these early Dutch imports were from Utrecht, rather than Flanders, and were "slow, heavy unwieldy animals . . . but capable of improvement in the direction of speed." But interestingly enough, nowhere in Wallace, Hervey, or any other Standardbred source I used, is the Harddraver mentioned.

On the other hand, in her book *Horses of the World*, in which she barely discusses this at all, Daphne Machin Goodall casually remarks that the Dutch Harddraver was a very old breed of trotter, and thereby, of course, she supplies us with an intriguing clue. What, after all, could be more reasonable? The little English pacers, crossed with slightly larger Dutch trotters, would most likely have resulted in a fine type of trotter-pacer. And that is precisely the result that was achieved.

In any event, Harddraver or no Harddraver, while all this was going on the Puritan colonies of Massachusetts were proving *too* Puritan and intolerant for Roger Williams and his followers. He and his whole congregation, then, left in disgust (or were driven out) and founded their own colony in Rhode Island in 1636. They also, being far more tolerant of such vices as fast horseflesh, founded the first truly American breed of horse, the widely renowned Narragansett Pacer.

Since "trade and commerce" were at that time rather successfully prohibited with the Dutch, the people around Narragansett Bay in Rhode Island had for their foundation stock only those horses that had been imported from England into Massachusetts. These were primarily pacers, but because of the religious feelings of the Massachusetts colonists—which forbade racing of any kind, they were not developed for nor noted for any particular amount of speed. Some selective breeding in that direction, however, along with pacing races and prizes to promote them, developed speed with amazing rapidity. By 1690, the Narragansett Pacer was not only an established type, but such a superior pacer that the demand for it extended to all the colonies and to the West Indies and Cuba. In fact, it was the Rhode Island Colony's principal export and its greatest claim to fame.

This Narragansett Pacer, remember, was highly valued as a swift, hardy, easy-gaited *saddler*. Since there were no roads yet in the colonies that were much more than packed-down Indian trails, this kind of horse was treasured here as it had once been in England. And, as Hiram Woodruff reminded us, the Narragansett Pacer was an ambler "at moderate speeds." Its immense popularity, as in England, lasted until roads were improved enough for vehicular traffic. Then it gradually moved westward as new frontiers were settled, until even those frontiers had good roads, and at last it disappeared altogether. But not before it played a substantial part, with its valuable pacing-ambling blood, in the creation of the American Saddle Horse, the Tennessee Walking Horse, the Missouri Fox Trotting Horse—and of course, the Standardbred.

The breed was, as we said, the first truly American horse breed, and it had already attained the peak of its glory before the Darley Arabian had even reached England, so it by far pre-dates the Thoroughbred. The average Narragansett Pacer seems to have been a bit over 14 hands high. Again, this seems terribly small, but nonetheless it was nearly a hand higher than the average Virginia horse of the same period. (And people were also smaller then than now, remember.)

The Hall of Fame of the Trotter (formerly Goodtime Stable) at Goshen, N.Y. houses the Harness Horse Museum and an extensive library.

On this general subject of the gait of the colonial horses of this period, Wallace dug up a copy of the *Boston News-Letter* of 1705. In it he found several notices of horses lost, strayed or stolen, and he reported the following examples: "Strayed or stolen: fourteen hands high, hardly possible to make him gallop," and "fourteen hands high, paces, trots and gallops."

Then, in 1731 and 1732: "black mare, fourteen and three-quarter hands, trots and paces," "bay horse, large, good pacer," "roan mare, fourteen hands, trots and paces." He further found that in 1777 and 1778, "the horses averaged about fourteen hands and one inch... and in the gaits of those advertised, fifteen both paced and trotted, nine trotted only, and seven paced only." These examples probably fairly represent the bulk of the American horse stock during the century from 1650 to 1750.

From this basic stock, by now considered "native," several different strains began to emerge. Down South and "out West" (Kentucky and Tennessee) the

*Messenger, a stallion imported in 1788, has the distinction of being extremely influential in the development of both the Standardbred and the Thoroughbred, as well as vastly improving general transportation.

saddle-gaited horses would soon dominate. But up North, where there began to be navigable roads, light-harness horses were developed. In puritan New England, especially, riding for "pleasure" was considered sinful, not to mention racing. Harness horses became the only respectable kind to own. So while most of the horse racing enthusiasts of the South and a few in New York were importing specimens of the new English running horse, beginning with Bulle Rock in 1730, the New Englanders and most New Yorkers disdained these "hothouse flowers" and remained loyal to their all-purpose utility horses—the pacers and trotters. Some of this was due to religious beliefs, some to practicality, and some, one suspects, to pure Yankee stubbornness.

It was one of those hot house flowers, however, an English Thoroughbred stallion named Messenger, who was almost entirely responsible for turning these good road horses into race horses, and for making the American road horse exceptionally speedy at the trot, as well as at the pace. The Americans already had the basic pacing blood, and with the arrival of Messenger, with his "distinctive power to transmit trotting speed," the future of the Standard-bred race horse was assured.

4

MESSENGER

Messenger was a Thoroughbred, or what passed for a Thoroughbred in 1780, the year he was foaled. That was only 16 years after the foaling of the great Eclipse, the horse often referred to as "the first Thoroughbred," so that breed was still very much in the nebulous stage that all new breeds start out in. Pacing blood had long been in disfavor in that country by then, especially in running horse pedigrees, and also frowned upon was trotting blood, which Messenger carried in plenty.

Messenger was a vital force as a breeding stallion, however, partly because of that very blood. After he was imported into Philadelphia in 1788 he went on to become extremely influential as a Thoroughbred sire of running race horses, but he was also the principal founder of the brand-new Standardbred line. It was, of course, his pedigree that made such a remarkable feat possible, with its strong undercurrents of trotting blood. Doubtless this unpopular aspect of his breeding was also responsible for his being exiled to the colonies in the first place. But here it was far from unpopular and was soon, in fact, recognized as a rare blessing.

Messenger's dam is not known for certain, although she is said to have been a mare by Turf, an early-Thoroughbred type. But Messenger's sire line *is* known, and provides more than ample food for thought. He was sired by Mambrino, a horse that went back to the Darley Arabian through Engineer, Sampson, Blaze, and Flying Childers. The female relatives of many of these stallions are unknown, but it is certain that there was some kind of pacing/trotting blood in this pedigree.

The period during which these horses were foaled, from the Darley's son Flying Childers (the most famous race horse of his time, known as "Mile-a-Minute Childers"), foaled in 1715, until Messenger in 1780, was one of Oriental supremacy in English horse breeding. The English race horse was still so close to its Oriental infusions by 1780 that it stood no more than 15 hands high, sometimes even under 14 hands, and was of the "desert-blooded," deerlike, small-headed conformation.

An advertisement for the services of the recently imported *Messenger is typical of the stud ads of the time.

It is quite evident that in Messenger's line, therefore, from Blaze onward in particular, there was more than the fashionable amount of native English blood of the larger, coarser, trotting type. The line was in fact noted for its "lack of the true running type" and was consequently shunned by fastidious race horse breeders. When Blaze's son Sampson, a heavy-boned horse standing a "phenomenal" 15.2 hands, was brought to the Malton race course, the joke of the day was "the coach horse here to run for the plate." The "coach horse," carrying 140 pounds, won the race in its first two 3-mile heats, and went on to keep winning similar races.

Sampson's son, Engineer, was of the same type—large, strong, and coarse, and so was Engineer's son, Mambrino, foaled in 1768. He was a "great, strong-boned grey horse" bred in Yorkshire. On his dam's side he evidently went back to the Bald Galloway through Cade and Roxana. And in Mambrino the old pacing/trotting blood came to the fore with a vengeance. As a sire of running horses he was a relative failure. But, according to the second volume of Pick's Turf Register, printed in 1805, "Mambrino was likewise sire of a great many excellent hunters and strong, useful road horses. And it has been said that from his blood the breed of horses for the coach was brought nearly to perfection." This is significant. Road horses and coach horses in England at that time were big, bold-going trotters. The very same statement could one day be made about Mambrino's descendants in the New World, through his fabulous son Messenger.

Before turning to Messenger, however, one must make note of the fact that Blaze, who sired Sampson, "the coach horse come to race," also sired a horse called Shales, or Old Shales. Shales was another vital progenitor of English trotting coach horses, and a foundation sire of the trotting Hackney breed. And Bellfounder, a Hackney descendant of Shales, when imported into the New World, became the sire of the dam of Hambletonian 10, "the father of the Standardbred."

This intriguing situation, Wallace reported, was summed up neatly by Henry F. Euren, compiler of the English Hackney Stud Book: "The fact that in the seventh generation from Blaze, on each side, the reunion of the blood in Rysdyk's Hambletonian, the sire of so many fast American trotting horses . . . would appear to warrant the conclusion that there was a strong latent trotting tendency in the near ancestors, on one, if not both, sides of Blaze." Indeed so — perhaps, in fact, it is *Blaze* that deserves the title of "father of the Standardbred!"

This trotting tendency of Blaze's, as it happened, was far from latent in his great-grandson Mambrino. Not only was Mambrino a great sire of coach horses, his owner was reported to have offered to trot him 14 miles an hour for a thousand guineas. And while as far as it is known the offer was never taken up, it is unlikely that it would have been made had not Mambrino "shown a good lick or two" at that gait, which is highly unusual in a running race horse.

Therefore, we can probably assume that some of those unknown mares behind Blaze, Sampson, and Mambrino were fairly large, a bit coarse, and pretty good trotters. Their descendants certainly were quality trotters, at any rate, and speed at the trot doesn't evolve overnight.

However, Messenger, Mabrino's most illustrious son, was a fair-to-middling running horse who never showed any propensity toward fast trotting, and he certainly didn't pace. When he was imported and bred on "Thoroughbred" mares he produced outstanding race horses. He was limited in that direction, since he spent most of his life near New York City in a period when running races were in disfavor there. But in spite of this severe obstacle he sired Miller's Damsel, who produced American Eclipse. Both Thoroughbreds became so famous and popular that they brought back running races almost all by themselves. Messenger's great contributions to the American Thoroughbred have nearly been forgotten now but they don't deserve to be.

He is much more renowned for the startling results that were attained when he was bred to "good road mares"—mares that paced and trotted. These numerous progenies, soon burning up the roads in New York and environs, were highly prized. They were called "Messengers," and so prepotent was this gray stallion that the "Messengers" were nearly a breed unto themselves.

It is not known who the breeder of Messenger was. By the time he was a three-year-old, in 1783, he was owned by the proprietor of a professional racing stable in Newmarket. He won some races from 1783 to 1785, mostly shorter ones, but he also lost some. The fact that he was not exactly a superhorse on the English race courses is evidenced by the fact that nothing more is known about him until he turned up in Philadelphia in 1788, advertised, of course, as a horse with a "so very great" racing record. The ad, unfortunately, does not mention who imported and/or owned the gray stallion then, and while various stories have been given credence from time to time, this is still really unknown. His stud fee, the ad says, was "a very low price of three guineas each mare, and one dollar to the groom." It adds boastfully that Messenger's sire Mambrino "covered at twenty-five guineas the leap," which makes his son a real bargain.

What did this newly imported English stallion look like? He was, as has been noted, a gray, and became lighter with age. He was true to his family line in that he was very large for his day at 15.3, and Wallace noted that

for a thoroughbred, his appearance was coarse. He did not supply the mind with an idea of beauty, but he impressed upon it a conception of solidity and power. His head was large and bony, with a nose that had a decided Roman tendency, though not to a marked degree. His nostrils were unusually large and flexible, and when distended they were enormous. ... His ear was larger than usual in the blood horse, but thin and tapering—and always active and expressive. The windpipe was unusually large and stood out... as a distinct feature. His neck was very short for a blood horse, but was not coarse and thick like a bull's... His withers were low and

MESSENGER, THE GREAT PROGENITOR (1780-1808)

CURRIER and IVES PRINT COURTESY of HARRY T. PETERS' COLLECTION
IMPORTED MESSENGER
THE GREAT FOUNTAIN HEAD·IN AMERICA· OF "MESSENGER BLOOD"
FOALED 1780, GOT BY MAMBRINO, HE BY ENGINEER, HE BY SAMPSON
HE BY BLAZE, HE BY FLYING CHILDERS, HE BY THE FAMOUS DARLEY
ARABIAN. MESSENGER'S DAM WAS BY TURF, HE BY MATCHEM,
HE BY CADE, HE BY THE GREAT GODOLPHIN ARABIAN, AND
THE SIRE OF THE DAM OF MESSENGER'S DAM WAS ALSO BY
THE GODOLPHIN ARABIAN.

HARNESS RACING FAMILY	RUNNING FAMILY
AMERICAN MAMBRINO	MILLER'S DAMSEL (F)
ABDALLAH	AMERICAN ECLIPSE
HAMBLETONIAN 10	MEDOC
	MELODY (F)
ELECTIONEER	FLORINE (F)
	AEROLITE (F)
CHIMES	SPENDTHRIFT
THE ABBE	HASTINGS
	FAIR PLAY
ABBEDALE	MAN O'WAR
HAL DALE	WAR ADMIRAL
	IRON MAIDEN (F)
DALE FROST	IRON REWARD (F)
	SWAPS
MEADOW SKIPPER	
⇧	**CHATEAUGAY**
(1960) WORLD CHAMPION THREE-YEAR-OLD PACER, 1:55⅗ FOR THE MILE	⇧
	(1960) 1963 KENTUCKY DERBY WINNER.
STRAIGHT LINE OF MALE DESCENDANCY, 11 GENERATIONS BACK TO MESSENGER.	16 GENERATIONS BACK TO MESSENGER INCLUDING SIX FEMALE DESCENDANTS.

*These charts show plainly how *Messenger's lines have "come down through the ages"
in both our racing breeds.*

round, which appears to have been a family characteristic, back for three generations at least. His shoulders were heavy and altogether too upright for our ideas of a
racehorse... His hips and quarters were 'incomparably superior to all others'... the
bones of Messenger's limbs were unusually large and strong for those of a thoroughbred. His pasterns and feet were all that could be desired, and as an evidence of the
excellence and health of his underpinning several writers have put it on record
that... he never was known to mopingly rest one leg by standing on the other three,
but was always prompt and upright.

This, then, was Messenger, forerunner of the American trotting-bred horse.
He was a Thoroughbred, by somewhat shaky record, but he was not typical of
the ideal Thoroughbred of his time, by any means. As to his temperament, it
was so waspish that stories circulated "about his killing his keepers." Wallace
thought this unlikely, as a "psychopathic" horse certainly wouldn't have
enjoyed such popular patronage among mare owners, but he does say that it is
"known with certainty that he was willful and vicious and would tolerate no
familiarity from strangers." This disposition would later be very pronounced
in some of his get and, in particular, in his grandson Abdallah.

Messenger was offered at stud in various places (Philadelphia, New York,
Long Island, etc.) from 1788 through 1807. His last five seasons were all
around New York City and Long Island. His fee started at about $15, ranged
upward to $30 at times, and dropped down again to $15 during his last three
seasons. Because of the woeful state of record-keeping in those days we can't
know how many foals this great stallion sired. A great many, perhaps most, of
the mares brought to him were not owned by record-keeping breeding farms,
anyway, but were just fast road mares whose owners thought enough of them to
breed them to this relatively high-fee'd stallion.

On January 28, 1808, Messenger died on Long Island, at twenty-eight
years old. Wallace gives us a vivid description of this historic event in his
book, *The American Horse*, 1897:

> This date has been as familiar to all intelligent horsemen for the last forty years as
> any prominent event in the history of the nation. The news of the death of the old
> patriarch spread with great rapidity, and soon the whole countryside was gathered
> to see the last of the king of horses and to assist at his burial. His grave was
> prepared at the foot of a chestnut tree some distance in front of the house, and there
> he was deposited in his holiday clothing. In response to the consciousness that a
> hero was there laid away forever a military organization was extemporized, and
> volley after volley by platoons was fired over his grave.

What had Messenger done that was so heroic? He had vastly improved the
road horses of his section of the country. And in those days, road horses were
vital. They provided family and personal transportation, business travel,
"light trucking," and in general the most indispensable segment of the
economy. Messenger's effect on all this was almost as though someone had

invented a faster, better-looking, longer-lasting car. The proud owner of a pair of Messengers felt much the same way as the owner of a smart, speedy sports car does today. When he flicked his whip over those powerful, "incomparably superior" hindquarters, he knew he'd better hold onto his hat!

Messenger's value to the American trotter-to-be was recognized early here, even though he was also, and was intended to be, a Thoroughbred sire. As early as 1866 Hiram Woodruff, the great trainer, wrote the following comment, with its prediction about the descendants of Messenger:

> Little attention as there has been paid to the cultivation of the trotting tendency in England, I find that there have been some thoroughbred trotters there, and some that were nearly thoroughbred. A gentleman who is well informed in the matter tells me that a large number of the horses sired by Lord Grosvenor's Mambrino, the sire of Messenger, had the natural trotting gift. . . .
>
> I think that there is but little doubt of the fact, that the only infusion of the blood into the trotting-horse to be relied on to improve the latter as a whole ought to come from families, who, as thoroughbreds, have shown a disposition to bend the knee, and trot. Those having a strong dash of Messenger blood would be apt to succeed; and it has succeeded in some notable instances.

And it certainly had, the *most* "notable instance" being Hambletonian, "the father of the Standardbred."

5

THE MORGANS

The Morgan line is certainly not a vastly important or enduring part of the story of the Standardbred, but it is an interesting and colorful one, due mainly to the tremendous amount of mystery and controversy surrounding its "founding father," the original Morgan horse, Justin Morgan.

The story most often seen in modern books dealing with the origin of the Morgan goes about like this:

Justin Morgan (the man of that name) was a poor but honest schoolteacher who lived in West Springfield, Massachusetts until he moved to Randolph, Vermont in 1788—the same year Messenger arrived in Philadelphia. In 1795, he returned to Springfield to collect a debt, receiving two colts in lieu of cash, a three-year-old gelding and a two-year-old bay stud colt, which he called Figure. This Figure, it is generally assumed, was the horse that later was named after his owner, and was the "original Morgan horse," a freak or mutant, unlike his parents but extremely prepotent in passing his own unique characteristics on to all his get. His dam is unknown, the story usually goes, but his sire was a Thoroughbred named Beautiful Bay and/or True Briton, a race horse stolen from a Tory during the Revolution. So much for "the story known to every school child."

Well, let's see. As far as the first Morgan's dam is concerned, she was evidently a local mare said to have been sired by Diamond, an imported English horse. She is also said to have been a chunky light bay, with a heavy mane and tail and heavily feathered legs. She sounds, in fact, rather like a miniature draft horse, and not especially unlike her son.

As to "Figure," as it is now widely believed that Mr. Morgan called his bay colt: Mr. Morgan, while he *was* apparently a poor but honest schoolteacher, also had a couple of sidelines to help feed his family. One was keeping a roadhouse, and the other was keeping stallions. Owners of stallions often sent them "out of town" for a few seasons, in the charge of some local man who kept part of the fees as payment. But our story becomes complicated by the evidence that while Morgan did keep a stallion for a year or two that was named Figure, he was advertised as "the famous horse Figure, from Hartford." "The Morgan horse" did not come from Hartford, nor was he then famous, so these were evidently two different stallions.

Most of the evidence seems to show that Justin Morgan (equine variety) was foaled in 1793. The very best evidence is the fact that "he was sold and resold and sold again, as a foal of 1793, and the date never left him till he died in 1821," according to Wallace. A young horse's age is plainly printed on its teeth, and any prospective buyer would surely have checked. So it seems positive to me that this horse was indeed foaled in 1793. It was only many years later, when all the maneuvering began to prove otherwise, that this date was even questioned. This is important, because the stallion True Briton seems to have been in Mr. Morgan's care in the spring of 1785, far too early for him to have sired the first Morgan horse.

On the other hand, further evidence shows that in the spring of 1792, in Springfield, Massachusetts, a stallion was advertised as follows: "Young Bulrock is a horse of the Dutch breed, of a large size, and a bright bay color . . . " Remember that "large" at that time, could mean as small as 14.2 hands. Remember also that the Dutch horses were comparatively "chunky and hairy," completely unlike the English blood horse of the time, which was Barb-like, fine-coated and slender.

The date for Young Bulrock is right, the place is right, and the conformation is right—even the color is right—for him to have been the sire of Justin Morgan. And, as Wallace remarked, "It is impossible to make a thinking and sensible man believe that a little hairy-legged 'nubbin' of a pony, weighing 850 pounds, hired for $15 a year to drag logs together in a clearing, at which employment he was a great success, had the blood of the race horse in his veins."

But of course *stranger* things have happened, including sports, freaks and mutants that breed on, and everyone is entitled to an opinion. My own is that Wallace was probably right, and that Justin Morgan was sired by Young Bulrock, especially since Mr. Morgan himself always referred to this stallion as "a Dutch horse." If that is so, and his dam was as described, then Justin Morgan was not a mutant that possessed astonishing prepotency to impress his own traits on his get—he was merely breeding true to his inherited type.

This widely-touted "prepotency" is perhaps the strangest part of the Morgan story, as well as the part most stressed. Because it actually seems only to have been true when they were bred to one another or to similar types. By about 1850, when the Morgans were at their peak of popularity, selling for high prices all over, it was noticed that when they were bred to a completely different type all Morgan characteristics were lost. This outbreeding was frequently attempted, in the hope of speeding them up—they were chunky, stylish, trappy-moving little things, with "little, short, quick steps . . . that gave them all the sensations of going fast, without the danger incident to rapid traveling"—but while the results of such out-crosses were faster and longer-striding, they were no longer "Morgans."

By the turn of the century, in fact, they were all but bred out completely. The subsequent establishment of the government-sponsored Morgan breeding farm in Vermont eventually brought them back, fortunately. This was accom-

*Hambletonian 10, a great-grandson of *Messenger and "the father of the modern Standardbred" exemplifies the adage "pretty is as pretty does."*

plished with the help of American Saddle Horse blood, which owed the Morgans something, anyway, for their early contribution to that breed.

That Justin Morgan was a great little horse, whatever his pedigree may have been, is without doubt. Messengers and Morgans were for a long time the "kings of the roads," and, as splendid cavalry mounts, they fought valiantly through at least three wars. When I remarked at the beginning of this chapter that the Morgan line was not vastly important to the Standardbred, I did not mean that it had no value at all. The Morgans were not fast trotters, and as far as is known, they did not pace. But they did have one very important trait— they had endless "bottom," as endurance and courage were called. And particularly in the early days of trotting races, when three and four-mile heats were common and races sometimes went on into the gloom of night, "bottom' was a most essential attribute. Where Morgan blood was used, it also contributed a much-needed stylishness and prettiness to the new breed.

Old Justin Morgan's death, at twenty-eight years old in 1821, was not heralded and mourned like Messenger's had been thirteen years earlier. He was not ceremoniously interred in his holiday clothing and no solemn volleys rang out. He died alone in a pasture, from the effects of a neglected kick wound.

He left several fine sons to carry on his heritage, but the only one that produced a line of trotters comparable to the Messengers was Sherman Morgan.

Sherman Morgan was a tiny horse, no more than 14 hands high, a typey Morgan of a bright chestnut hue that was foaled in 1809. His dam was a "high class Narragansett pacer." He was not a great trotter, and his name would now be unknown (except to Morgan enthusiasts) had he not been credited with siring a great trotter, named Black Hawk.

A controversy arose, and raged on for years, over the true paternity of Black Hawk, because Black Hawk was a large, beautiful horse that did not resemble the Morgan type in any way. Nor have any of his descendants. This controversy probably wouldn't have been so bitter or so enduring had it not been for the economics involved. The plain fact was that the New England breeders whose Morgan colts and fillies *were* of the true Morgan type were losing sales to breeders of the Black Hawks. The latter were larger, faster, could really trot, were altogether more salable, and salable at an earlier age. So the contention that Black Hawk was not a Morgan at all is understandable. Those other breeders also had a reason besides his non-Morgan appearance and action to bolster their suspicion, for Sherman Morgan's owner had been the object of a "paternity suit" over just that very suspicion.

After studying several differing versions of this paternity suit story, I have come up with this one as the most likely-seeming one:

In 1832, Benjamin Kelly owned a black mare called Old Narragansett. He also owned a tavern in Durham, New Hampshire. One of the tavern's customers was a Mr. Bellows, who would stop there in his seasonal rounds with his two stallions, Sherman Morgan and Paddy, a little black stud. Kelly's black pacer was bred to Sherman Morgan, whose stud fee was $14. The apparently inferior Paddy's fee was an even more modest $7. After this mating, Old Narragansett was sold to one Shade Twombley, a neighboring citizen, who agreed to pay Mr. Bellows the stud fee should the mare produce a living foal.

In due course, in the spring of 1833, she did just that. But the foal, a little black colt, did not strike Mr. Twombley as being a Morgan. So he paid Mr. Bellows only $7 instead of $14, since he believed (or said he believed) that the black Paddy must have actually been Old Narragansett's consort, and not the bright red Sherman. Seven dollars being seven dollars in those days, when a common stud fee might be a bushel of corn, and with his integrity being questioned, Mr. Bellows stuck by his guns and the lawsuit ensued. Twombley lost, and he also died, so his estate had to pay the extra seven dollars. To this day, there are many who are still convinced that the famous Black Hawk line, prominent in American Saddle Horse, Tennessee Walking Horse, and Standardbred beginnings, had nothing to do with Morgans, although Black Hawk's Sherman Morgan pedigree is given as accepted fact in the various breed registries in which it appears.

In a way, the die-hards are right, because as Wallace pointed out, even if we assume that Sherman Morgan was truly the sire of Black Hawk, Black Hawk was still only about 25% Morgan. Sherman Morgan's dam was a Narragansett Pacer, which makes him half Morgan. Black Hawk's dam was also a Narragansett Pacer, who was "tall, breedy," and weighed 1100 pounds. She was well-known locally as an exceptionally fast trotter, and paced (or ambled) under saddle. Her exact breeding was unknown, but she was recognized by everyone who saw her as a well-bred mare of striking appearance and ability. Therefore, not to denigrate the Morgan blood's contribution here, the fact remains that Black Hawk was a 75% Narragansett, and that was the only "Morgan" that ever founded a line of really fast trotters.

As to Black Hawk himself, he was such a marvelous looking horse—about 15 or 15.1 hands high, coal black, and beautifully formed—that he became almost the nation's ideal horse. In her book, "The Morgan Horse," Jeanne Mellin stated that Black Hawk was always a square trotter. Wallace, on the other hand, said that "Black Hawk's gait was spluttery and uneven, rather than square and mechanical," which one might expect, perhaps, from so much pacing blood. Whichever, he was apparently very fast. Three of his get managed to do a 2:30 or better mile, which in those days was fairly rare.

The rest of the Morgans instrumental in the development of the Standardbred, like Daniel Lambert and the Morrills, while possessed of Morgan blood, might just as well be called Messengers or something else. No nearly-pure Morgan ever possessed great speed at the trot, apparently, or produced it. Nonetheless, with most of our best Standardbreds eventually tracing back to Justin Morgan—some of them many times—it is a significant factor in the history of the trotting-bred horse. One of its family members, Black Hawk's son Ethan Allen, became the most enduring national favorite the country had ever seen.

6
HAMBLETONIAN

Messenger reached America in 1788, Justin Morgan died in 1821, and Black Hawk was foaled in 1833. These dates will give you something to hang this next date on—1849. One of the most important dates in Standardbred history, it was the year that "the father of them all" was foaled. His name was Hambletonian, and it is doubtful that there are more than a handful of harness race horses now living that are *not* descended from Hambletonian.

Hambletonian was definitely a "Messenger," and, as we mentioned earlier, he was also a "Blaze," on both sides. In fact, as Wallace said, Hambletonian had more real trotting blood behind him than any other horse of his generation. How this blood happened to be combined in this one fantastic stallion is a fascinating story.

Hambletonian's sire was Abdallah, a grandson of Messenger through the Thoroughbred Mambrino—not to be confused with Messenger's *sire* Mambrino, the English horse. It is widely accepted now after a great deal of argument, that Abdallah's dam, Amazonia, was a grand-daughter of Messenger, which makes Abdallah inbred to Messenger. Amazonia had "coarse, ragged hips," a "rat tail," was a "muddy sorrel" in color, and had "hair enough on her legs to stuff a mattress." So much for the bad news. The good news is that she was considered "phenomenally fast" at the trot.

Abdallah, her offspring, was no beauty, either, although he was at least "in color a beautiful bay," and he did have a fine, lustrous coat. But he was considered coarse and homely (he had his mother's rat tail, too) and disregarding his other faults, he had an ungovernable temper that reminded people of Messenger on his worst days. When an attempt at training him to harness was made, it was soon found to be a foolhardy experiment and all his long life he never willingly allowed leather to touch his back. This ugliness of temper and conformation proved to be his undoing. After being kept at stud near New York City for a few years, in 1839 he was sent to Kentucky. He only made one season there, as trotting-breds were still not much accepted in the Blue Grass and even if they had been, Kentucky horsemen liked their horses to be beautiful. They sent Abdallah right back to Long Island after he had sired only six Kentucky foals.

His different owners then placed him at stud at various places near New York City again for several years, his progenies doing very well on the trotting tracks in that vicinity. Then when he was past his usefulness, his unsentimental owner sold him for a few dollars to a Long Island fish peddler, to pull his cart. But, incorrigible as ever, the old horse promptly kicked harness and cart into as small pieces as possible. At that point the disgusted peddler simply turned him out onto a barren beach to fend for himself as best he could. And here again we have a description of a great horse's passing, written by a famous portraitest of race horses, Henry H. Cross:

> In November 1854, it happened that I was at the Union Course sketching a horse... when a man drove in, bringing the news that old Abdallah had just been found dead on Gravesend Beach. I accordingly drove over with other horsemen to get a last look at this celebrated stallion. The sight that met our eyes was indeed a grewsome one. The old horse had run loose in the wind and weather in the fall, subsisting as best he could upon beach and marsh grass and such other forage as he could pick up. Finally he had taken refuge in an old shanty on the beach, which he had grown too feeble to leave. There he had literally starved to death. He had died standing, game to the last. In his struggles he had dug a deep hole with his forefeet... and appeared as if half buried, his fore parts being three feet lower than his hind ones. He was, as I have said, on his feet, as he had never lain down. Instead he had leaned against the side of the shanty for support, and in that position had drawn his last breath. I can never forget the spectacle he presented. It was one of the most extraordinary and at the same time the most pathetic I have ever seen— his strange posture, his gaunt, skeleton-like frame covered with long woolly hair and the ghastly surroundings. I believe he was given a decent burial and his hoofs, his tail and some other portions of his anatomy were preserved.

Ghastly, indeed—and what a contrast to the ceremonial burial of Messenger. But how typical of Abdallah, to have kicked himself into such a situation, rather than submit to being a cart horse, and to have "died on his feet," fighting to the very end. This trait of Abdallah's would be noticed later in some of his descendants, as we shall see.

The female side of Hambletonian's pedigree is not without its more remarkable elements, either. The Seely family, a numerous one, had long been noted as a family of canny horsemen in the very horse-oriented section of lower New York State known as Orange County. In 1801, Jonas Seely, Sr. bred his "great, slashing" black mare, Jin (breeding unknown), to Messenger. This, in 1802, produced a dark brown mare with white hairs in her tail, named Silvertail. This filly was Seely's first experience with Messenger blood, and he thought he could use more of the same, so in 1814, when Bishop's Hambletonian, a son of Messenger, came to Goshen in Orange County for a season, Silvertail was taken to him. The result of this inbreeding was another mare, who soon earned herself a reputation for willfulness and the name One Eye, gained when, in one of her tantrums, she lost an eye. She is said, by those who saw her, to have been wonderfully enduring and to have had a "grand open trotting step."

Wallace even went so far as to say that, "Right at this point and in this mare, One Eye, we have the incipient cause of all Hambletonian's greatness." She was a brown mare, over 15 hands high, with two white feet. During her lifetime One Eye had five or six foals, all apparently "willful," and one, her first, was a pacer.

Later in life she was sold to Josiah Jackson, also of Orange County, and in 1831 or 1832 she was bred to imported Bellfounder, the Hackney descendant of Blaze. Thus, as mentioned before, the two Blaze lines merged in One Eye's filly. Bellfounder had no great speed, but he *was* a "Norfolk trotter" and he had a fine trotting action. The result of One Eye's and Bellfounder's brief romance was a bay filly with three white ankles and a star, and the typical Messenger temperament. But she was large (15.3) and fast, and while her hips are described as rather coarse, she was powerful behind and had a comely head and neck. She was sold several times, each time at a nice profit, until she became half of a fast road team in New York City. Soon, however, her temperament flared up, resulting in a runaway and an accident that injured her severely.

She was then sold to a prosperous New York butcher, Charles Kent, and was thereafter known as the Kent Mare, or the Crippled Kent Mare. But Jonas Seely, Jr., hearing of her bad fortune, bought her back into the Seely family for $135 and returned her to Orange County in 1842.

There she had four foals before she was bred in 1848 to ugly old "fight to the finish" Abdallah, and in 1849 she produced the bay colt, Hambletonian. With all this obstreperous Messenger temperament on both sides of his family, Hambletonian was very lucky in that he "took after" his grand-dad, Bellfounder, who was a sweet-tempered, docile soul. It has been a source of endless speculation as to what else this bit of Bellfounder blood may have done for the Standardbred breed. It no doubt contributed "trotting blood," but the Kent Mare was the only really fast trotter he ever sired, and that appears to have been due primarily to her Messenger blood. Wallace concluded that "Bellfounder was a failure as a speed sire... and so were his sons." But Messenger was not, and Hambletonian was an intensely inbred Messenger.

Hambletonian's story is well known, and we will just go over it quickly. At the time that Jonas Seely, Jr. bred the Kent Mare to Abdallah, his hired man was William Rysdyk, a practically penniless man—but one with his eye open for a good, money-making investment. In those days, a good stallion was just such an investment, and when Rysdyk got a chance to buy both the Kent Mare and her new bay colt for $125 he jumped at it, even though he had to buy them "on time." And then he didn't waste a minute. He was advertising the bay colt at stud when he was only two years old. He got three foals that year, too, one of which was Alexander's Abdallah, the sire of the great Goldsmith Maid. As a three-year-old, Hambletonian sired thirteen foals. This was just the beginning of a long stud career that would eventually produce over 1300 foals.

As to their quality, and the quality of *their* children, this can best be shown by the fact that in two generations, Hambletonian and his get had produced 1,705 horses that could trot in 2:30 or better, the "standard" at that time! His nearest competitor was Blue Bull, whose 2:30 performers in two generations numbered a respectable but comparatively puny 271.

All his life Hambletonian belonged to William Rysdyk, who died before his famous horse did but who provided for him in his will. In appearance, Hambletonian greatly resembled that whole Blaze line, with its certain coarseness and its immense power. He was a mahogany bay with black legs, a small star, and both hind ankles white. His head was large and bony, and unlike the ideal blood horse, who could "drink water out of a tin cup," Hambletonian's muzzle, Wallace claimed, could not have fitted into a "vessel of much smaller dimensions than a half-bushel measure." His ears were big, and most often "lopped backward." He was four inches longer than he was tall (15.1,¼ hands high), and two full inches higher at the hips than at the withers—truly a trotting pitch! He had great depth at the heart and a large, heavily muscled chest, but it was his tremendous development of loin and hindquarters that really set him above all others, as it had Messenger, and that gave him his marvelous, elastic action and great stride. In general, he gave an impression of immense power, but certainly not of beauty. In fact, Wallace remarked, "His two great, meaty ends, connected with a long and perfect barrel, two or three sizes too small for the ends, showed such a marked disproportion that I often wondered at it." Another indication that Hambletonian was noticeably lacking in beauty is that he was often called "Rysdyk's Big Bull."

The idea now sometimes held that Hambletonian himself could not trot especially fast seems to be false. Rysdyk was a good businessman, and he often showed how fast his money-making stallion could trot at the Orange County fairs. As a three-year-old, he was timed in 2:48½, which was speedy for an undeveloped horse of that age in those times, and later it was contended by several knowledgeable horsemen who knew him that he could trot 2:40 any day he cared to. Hambletonian could trot, all right, and the best proof of that is the fact that as a four-year-old his book held 101 mares. Since at that time nobody trained race horses before they were at least four, and Hambletonian's get had yet to reach the tracks, he must have been a pretty good trotter, himself. When his get did begin to show their speed, of course, Rysdyk began taking in money with both hands—an estimated $200,000 altogether.

The Hambletonians soon replaced the Messengers as the reigning monarchs of the roads and streets, and the trappy little Morgans had to give way to the new kings, too. The Morgans were still valued as pretty, all-round family horses, but where speed was wanted they simply couldn't compete with Hambletonian's get and descendants. They didn't go out without a struggle, though, and the most renowned battle between the two lines was the great Dexter-Ethan Allen race, in 1867.

Hambletonian died in 1876 at the age of twenty-seven. Mr. Rysdyk having died before this, his wishes were carried out for him. Hambletonian was dressed in a "new suit of clothing made to measure," placed in a box, and buried in front of Rysdyk's house. Subsequently a large monument was built on the spot to mark the resting place of the first Standardbred.

7

HIRAM WOODRUFF'S ERA

The best eyewitness we have to the chaotic period in trotting racing prior to the famous Dexter-Ethan Allen match is the great trainer Hiram Woodruff. More than just a witness, he was an active participant. He was born in 1817 and died in 1867, being thirty-two years old when Hambletonian was foaled and of an age to be in the thick of things. At his death George Wilkes, the editor of *The Spirit of the Times*, wrote:

> ... the development of the American trotter to his present pre-eminence over all other breeds of horses used for harness and road purposes is more due to Hiram Woodruff than to any, if not to all other men who ever lived... he doubled the value of the original element on which he worked, and, at the end of a few years, gave a - *great* animal to the country, in place of what had only been a *good* animal before.

Charles J. Foster wrote of him: "The Woodruffs were a family of horsemen. The old Colonel was noted as a trainer. His brother, George Woodruff, was still more famous in that capacity, and was without an equal, except Peter Whelan, as a rider of trotting-horses, until his nephew appeared, and surpassed them both."

The word "rider" might seem inaccurate, but trotting races were mostly under saddle until, around 1850, they gradually changed over to harness. Hiram got his start, in fact, riding the famous horse Topgallant at his exercise for his uncle George. Anyone who has ridden a fast trotting horse, without posting, for any length of time will appreciate the exertion required, and readily believe that Hiram was a very athletic young man, noted for his strength. Horses were made of very tough material in those days, too, as witness the following description, by Foster again, of Hiram's first entry as a race rider:

> His first race was ridden at the Hunting-Park Course, Philadelphia, where George had Topgallant, Whalebone, Columbus, and others of great note, in training. The gentlemen who frequented the ground one afternoon offered a purse, to be trotted for by any horses the boys could pick up. Young Hiram (he was then

fourteen years old) knew that there was at plough in a field hard by a horse called Shaking Quaker, that had trotted on Long Island. This horse he got, and with him he won the purse. In two or three weeks it was followed by another race for a larger amount, Mr. F. Duffy having backed his mare Lady Kate to trot fifteen miles an hour. He selected Hiram and another boy to ride, never imagining that one of them could ride a fast trotter the whole hour without a rest. Duffy, in fact, played a keen game; for he led the mare up and down by the bridle, with a heavy saddle on, and induced the backers of time to believe that he was going to ride her himself. His money was well laid, and the time for the start was near, when the backers of the watch, to their surprise and confusion, saw little Hiram come out of the bushes, with his light saddle on his arm, to ride the mare. She trotted sixteen miles in a trifle less than fifty-seven minutes.

Sixteen miles per hour, as a *rate* of speed, for a mile or two, is not fast, of course. But sixteen miles *in* an hour—nearly a whole hour—is quite a feat, for both horse and rider, especially since as the hour wore on and the horse began to tire, it would more and more lay on the bit, requiring ever more effort from the rider to balance and steady it. Hiram was to accomplish many such grueling "time-trials" in his life, and he was soon famous country-wide for his tremendous ability.

As a further example of the kind of races, and the kind of horses and riders, in the early 1800s, Hiram himself gives us a valuable insight by describing a three-mile heat race in Philadelphia in 1831 in which his Uncle George, who had a training stable, had entered three horses, among them the twenty-four-year-old gelding Topgallant, a horse that, moreover, was spavined in both hind legs! He relates the scene:

Thus there were eight trotters in the race: Dread, ridden by George Spicer; Topgallant, ridden by Matt Clintock in the first three heats, and by Uncle George Woodruff in the fourth; Collector, ridden by Peter Whelan; Chancellor, ridden by Frank Duffy; Whalebone, ridden by Frank Tolbert in the first two heats, but in the third by George Woodruff; Lady Jackson, ridden by John Vanderbilt; Moonshine, by James Hammil; and Columbus, by George Woodruff, until he broke down in the second heat. Dread was a handsome bay gelding, about fifteen hands and an inch, a beautiful goer, and a horse of capital bottom. Columbus was a bright bay horse, sixteen hands high... Chancellor was a handsome dapple gray, with a long tail. At that time most of our horses were docked. He was about fifteen hands two inches, and had a deal of style... Lady Jackson was a red gray mare, fifteen hands and half an inch high. She was quite handsome. Moonshine was a dark gray gelding, fifteen hands and half an inch high, with a long tail. He was a fine, stylish horse.

The odds at the start for the first heat was on Columbus, a hundred to seventy against the field. It was one of the finest sights I ever saw when these eight splendid bays and grays, all in the finest order, and their jockeys in the richest and most varied colors and beautiful costumes, came thundering along for the word, in a group, at the flying trot. Eight such horses and such riders had never met before, and it is doubtful when they will again. Never, certainly, until the good old customs of using trotting-horses under saddle, and requiring jockeys to ride them, are revived.

At the period I speak of, and prior to that, the riders of the trotters had always to be dressed in jockey costume for the race; and there was a great deal of expense and taste laid out in the rich velvets and silks of vivid hue, of which the jackets and caps were made up. The word being given, away they went for the first heat of three miles; Collector had the speed of the party. Columbus did not go as well as usual… Collector won the heat with great ease in 8:16; and… Peter Whelan said afterwards that he could have distanced the whole of the others, in his opinion, if his party had let him go along. The next heat was won by old Topgallant; and in this Columbus broke down. Thereupon, George Woodruff mounted Whalebone for the third heat.

The excitement was very great, and away they went again. This time Dread won; and Whalebone, not having won a heat in three, was ruled out. Now, then, George Woodruff mounted old Topgallant for the last struggle. At that time there was no rule against having more than one horse entered and started in a race of heats from the same stable. In this race we had three—Topgallant, Whalebone, and Columbus; and such were the vicissitudes and fortunes of the day, that, before it was over, my uncle had ridden all three. The only horses that had won a heat were Collector, Topgallant, and Dread; and, of course, these alone came to the post for the fourth heat, the great riders, Peter Whelan, George Woodruff, and George Spicer, being on them respectively. The veteran of twenty-four years, old Topgallant, went away under full sail, and led them for two miles and some two or three hundred yards; but Dread then came along and passed him, and won the deciding heat easily.

These horses, it will be perceived, trotted twelve miles; and here was old Topgallant, beaten in the race, it is true, but winner of a heat, and second in the last heat, thus getting second place in the race. The following week, after this great race at Philadelphia, we went to Baltimore, where they gave a purse of three hundred dollars, three-mile heats. Topgallant and Whalebone contended for it… Topgallant won it. This shows the tremendous endurance and recuperative energy of that wonderful horse's constitution. One week a very hard race of four three-mile heats, against all the best horses of the day; the next week another race of three-mile heats against Whalebone; and this Topgallant won easily, being, as I have before said, but which cannot too often be repeated, in his twenty-fourth year.

Topgallant was twenty-eight when he died.

This is as typical a trotting race of the period as can be found, and while these horses were the "cracks" of their day, they too are typical. Three-mile, or even four-mile heats were most common, and the races often went on into the night or were held over to be finished the following day. A trotting-horse's annual campaign consisted of many such races, sometimes only a few days apart, and when he traveled from one meet to another—from Long Island to Philadelphia or Boston—he got there on his own four feet. Moreover, a trotter was expected to continually improve as he got older and be at his best speed and "bottom" when in his teens. But he was thoroughly prepared for such an arduous life. Long, slow, careful work, not begun until the horse was at least four-years-old—and many of the best trotters of the day were not even harnessed until they were six or eight-years-old—got them into such splendid condition and kept them there. These races, remember, were fully intended to be tests of "bottom" just as much as of speed. Speed did a road horse little good if he played out before the end of the journey was reached.

As these things often do, however, it occasionally got out of hand. In 1856, Henry William Herbert, under the pen-name of Frank Forester, wrote the first serious book on American horses, in two volumes containing over one thousand pages. In this significant work, he mentioned several recent "barbarous matches," including one he had just read about in "The Spirit of the Times:"

"The spotted mare Anna Bishop was backed to do one hundred miles in nine hours; she started, and, after doing forty-nine miles in four hours and eleven minutes, broke down." This sort of thing was considered and reported as "a grand performance," but, as Mr. Herbert said, they were actually "savage atrocities." It is to be hoped that they were either given up or outlawed before too many horses were killed.

Such horrifying marathons are not, however, to be compared with the three- and four-mile heat races. While certainly tests of endurance, these races were well within the capacities of the superbly conditioned, mature trotters of the times. Wise trainers said, "Early speed means early decay," and, under the conditions of the day, they were right. Now, when we race two- and three-year-olds, they are only asked to do one-mile dashes, for the most part, and while the present rule of retiring a harness horse at fifteen might have meant "early decay" to Hiram Woodruff, whose trotters were often setting new marks regularly at that age, to today's horsemen it is virtual senility. Different horses for different times. Nowadays, very few people, with the exception of certain religious groups, are interested in good road horses, and with harness racing purely a sport, it simply doesn't matter if a horse can pull 300 or 400 pounds for twelve miles at top speed, and do it for 15 or 20 years. But it mattered very much a century ago.

During his supremely successful career, cut off so cruelly when he was only fifty years old, Hiram Woodruff rode, and later drove, the best trotters of his time, among them Dexter, Dutchman, and Flora Temple. His first really famous one was the bay gelding Dutchman, pedigree a complete mystery, who until he was five-years-old worked in a string of horses pulling a brick cart. Fortunately someone noticed that he could trot, his tail was "pricked and docked" and he was put in training. Dutchman was not only fast, but a good weight-puller, which was very important then, we must remember, if the race horse was to "improve the breed" of road horses. Dutchman's sulky weighed 82 pounds, and in the many wagon races of the day, a horse would be pulling about 350 pounds, an ordinary-sized driver included. Hiram admitted that "Dutchman was a little too rough in the stable, and, if not closely watched, was apt to take the jacket off a man's back at a mouthful," but he loved all his horses—one of the "secrets" of his great success in a time of great harshness.

8
ETHAN ALLEN AND DEXTER

We have already noted that Black Hawk was considered a representative of the Morgan line, even though he was actually only about 25% Morgan. He was the closest thing to a fast-trotting Morgan that Morgan breeders had to point to with pride. His son, Ethan Allen, was foaled the same year as Hambletonian, 1849, in Ticonderoga, New York, and he was "a handsome, bright bay horse, less than fifteen hands high." His dam was "a fast-trotting grey mare of unknown pedigree," according to Wallace, but according to Morgan horse fanciers, "said to be" by a little bay horse named Red Robin, who was "thought to be" by Justin Morgan, all of which may very well be true, and if it is, makes Ethan Allen much more of a Morgan representative than his sire Black Hawk was.

With his small stature, compact build, high head carriage, and thick, long mane and tail, Ethan Allen certainly looked more like a Morgan than anything else, although Hiram Woodruff, who knew the horse well, claimed that his dam was "a gray mare of the Messenger strain," and Herbert seems to agree. In any event, there is no question but that Ethan Allen was well loved. Even Wallace had to declare: "With a list of all the celebrated American horses before him, it would be very difficult, if not impossible [to select] an animal that has been so great a favorite with the American people, and for so long a time, as the famous Ethan Allen."

Hiram Woodruff remarked: "He stood very high in the New England states, because he was the chief representative of the Morgan line, and also the fastest stallion that had then been trained." As an example of Ethan Allen's tremendous standing in the eyes of the public, his image, cast in iron or bronze as a weather vane, trotted atop most of the houses and barns in the country, and there was literally no one over three years old in America who did not know the name "Ethan Allen."

59

From the time he was four-years-old he created one sensation after another, and when he was eighteen he was still at it, going a mile in 2:15 with a running mate. His speed, his beauty, his "remarkable docility and kindness," and his superb trotting action all combined to make him the nation's favorite horse for many years. "His trotting gait was recognized by all the best judges and experts as probably more perfect than that of any horse of his day," said Wallace. "Others have gone faster singly, but no one has done it in greater perfection of motion. In his great flights of speed he was not bounding in the air, but down close to the ground, with a gliding motion that steals from quarter pole to quarter pole with inconceivable rapidity." And in 1867, the eighteen-year-old Ethan Allen was matched against Dexter, the then nine-year-old gelded son of Hambletonian.

Dexter became nearly as popular as Ethan Allen had ever been, and as a Hambletonian, his feats did much to enhance his sire's already considerable reputation as a getter of fast trotters. He was bred in Orange County, and was a rich brown in color, with four white legs and a blaze, only an inch over fifteen hands high and "long for his inches" (longer than he was tall). "He was", Hiram said, "foaled in 1858 and not held in much favor for some time. His white legs and blaze set people against him. I have no doubt the old saw,—'One white leg, inspect him; Two white legs, reject him; Three white legs, sell him to your foes; Four white legs, feed him to the crows!'—was often quoted by people who saw this colt in the field at Mr. Hawkins'."

One man who saw the white-legged four-year-old brown colt in the pasture had no such prejudices, however. This was George B. Alley, a noted New York sportsman and one of the many "gentleman sports" who raced their fast horses on the streets and roads in and around New York City.

This seems rather amazing to us now, but for many years this group of wealthy New Yorkers was a positive menace with their fast pairs and four-in-hands. This sport was called road-riding, and while people from all classes had always brushed their best horses against one another, this New York clique was the elite of society, and wealthy enough to have its own way. They were also extremely influential in giving the developing new breed of road horse a tremendous boost. All of this is best explained and described by the following, written in 1904 by a member of the group, Hamilton Busbey:

> Road-riding movements quickened the development of the light-harness horse, but men of resolute purpose were required to lead in order to lift the horse into an atmosphere of respect. In 1856, when Robert Bonner first appeared on the road, trotting was in bad repute, and years of stern example were required to restore it to public favor. Burnham's, a house of refreshment on Bloomingdale Road and 76th Street, was the first rendezvous of gentlemen drivers, and Elm Park of the Bloomingdale Road at 92nd Street was the next resort. Admission to the club-house and half-mile track was restricted to members.... The first noted pair of Mr. Bonner were Flatbush Maid and Lady Palmer, and it was in the autumn of 1861 that he

drove these good mares around the Union Course in 2:27. ....Commodore Vanderbilt's pair were Post Boy and Plow Boy, and he was jealous of their reputation. The spirit of rivalry between Bonner and Vanderbilt grew more intense with the years, and their respective friends caught the fever, and breeders and trainers reaped the profit. Later John D. Rockefeller, William Rockefeller, Frank Work, William H. Vanderbilt, T. C. Eastman, and C. J. Hamlin were carried forward by the torrent, and the road-riding movement was at its zenith.

As these gentlemen drivers got more enthusiastic—and numerous—and as they acquired faster and faster teams, often trained by professional race drivers like Hiram Woodruff, Dan Pfifer, Dan Mace and Budd Doble, the streets and "lanes" of New York and the roads into Long Island became veritable raceways. The dangerous aspects of this fast, heavy traffic, combined with the usual resentment "common folk" feel toward the rich who flaunt their wealth, resulted in an uproar of indignation. When it is added that the New York bus drivers (horse-drawn buses, of course) seem to have "caught the fever," too, and to have been inordinately belligerent, as well, and the daily papers were full of vituperous remarks about buses forcing private vehicles onto the sidewalks, we can see that New York City streets, then, would make a modern-day taxi driver count his blessings. But even the wealthiest could not go on indefinitely running the rest of the populace off the roads, and the clamor for some kind of protection grew even louder. The solution to the problem—a "speedway" built just for these informal but intense races—came about in a typically arrogant fashion, as witness Mr. Busbey's report:

> The expansion of the city destroyed Harlem Lane for fast driving; and then at the suggestion of prominent road drivers I started an agitation for a speedway on the west side of Central Park. During the administration of Hugh J. Grant as Mayor of New York, a bill was passed by the legislature authorizing the construction of such a drive-way; but the opposition was so violent that the vote was reconsidered and the measure defeated. When Thomas F. Gilroy succeeded Mr. Grant as mayor, a bill for a speedway on the west bank of the Harlem River was prepared and passed by the legislature and signed by the governor. In the interest of this measure the Road Horse Association of the State of New York was formed, in 1892.

All of this sounds well and good, so far. It "gets them off the streets," and one would assume that these wealthy gentlemen would be paying for the construction of their speedway. But wait—in a letter to Mr. Busbey, concerning the controversy over whether the new speedway should include sidewalks, Robert Bonner wrote: "I do not see any objection to having two sidewalks on the speedway so long as all means of passage across it shall be by archways. It is true that the building of two sidewalks will involve greater expense, but as they are intended for the accommodation of the people, and the people have to pay for them, I do not see any good reason for depriving the public of the enjoyment to be derived from witnessing exhibitions of speed."

The "people"—the taxpayers who were footing the bills—would generously be allowed to watch, if they didn't get in the way.

Such was the situation when, in 1862, George Alley visited the Orange County farm and saw Dexter. Four hundred dollars later he owned the unbroken colt and took him home. Then followed several attempts by Mr. Alley to drive Dexter, and a few spills. "He jumps like a cat," Hiram tells us, and was a "high-strung, nervous, determined horse."

Then in the fall of 1863, about the time that the Battle of Chickamauga was raging down in Georgia, Dexter came to Hiram Woodruff for some real training. Hiram put him to a "wagon" shortly thereafter (these were racing wagons, very light, with extremely spidery, high wheels) and gave him a trial in 2:42. A week later, "in harness," (meaning to a two-wheeled sulky), Dexter pounded along in 2:31,1/4. At this point, Hiram remarks, "Here was indication of great speed when it should be developed, in course of time; and as he trotted the last halves of these miles as fast as he did the first, I set him down at once as possessed of bottom worthy of his breeding. Mr. Alley and I immediately concluded that in Dexter we had got hold of an extraordinary young horse."

Hiram Woodruff was not noted for overstating things, and he certainly wasn't that time. Mr. Alley took his promising colt home for the winter and then back to Hiram in the spring of 1864. He now was six-years-old and considered mature enough to be entered in some purses at the Fashion and Union Courses on Long Island. After a little more training, Dexter trotted his first race at Fashion in May for $100—mile heats, three out of five. His very first heat was indicative of what this "extraordinary young horse" had in store for the public. He won it by six lengths, "jogging," in 2:33. In the following two weeks, he trotted eleven heats—and was never even headed. People began to notice this white-legged "little big one" named Dexter.

That year and the next two occurred a series of heavily attended races, between Dexter and such other cracks as Lady Thorn, Flora Temple, and Stonewall Jackson. There was a particularly interesting match in 1865 between Dexter and Stonewall Jackson, under saddle. Stonewall was a fast horse, but temperamental, and known to bolt now and then. Hiram was getting a bit old and heavy for race-riding, so the great John Murphy rode Dexter in this match, with the equally famous Dan Mace up on Stonewall. It had been raining hard and the track, Hiram said, was "like a canal." As in all the races of those times, wet or dry, both horses made repeated breaks, and Dexter's breaks lost him the first heat. But then he got his mud legs, and "went on through the mud with his fine, square stroke, splashing away, seemingly as much at ease as a duck in a horse pond. Stonewall, on the contrary, was all abroad." Dexter won, as he did most of his races.

Meanwhile Ethan Allen, now well into his teens, had been setting records in a new way—with a running mate. This method stirred up much argument, as might be expected. The trotter was hitched in double harness with a runner, the harness being so rigged that the runner took most if not all of the weight. It was a fad, and didn't last too long, but while it did some relatively poor trotters put in some surprisingly good miles! As one driver explained it, "all the trotter had to do was to lay in the harness and keep his legs moving." Ethan Allen had made some very fast records this way, his best being 2:19,¾, and then Dan Mace took him over, trained him with Charlotte F. as his runner, and improved him even more.

Thus it was that Ethan's owner, Mr. Simmons, challenged the now-famous Dexter to trot singly against Ethan and Charlotte F. John Splan, one of the foremost drivers of the late 1800s, said that the public thought that "Mr. Simmons had over-matched his horse." Ethan was, of course, eighteen years old to Dexter's nine-year-old prime. Mr. Simmons, however, had so much confidence in his team that he "bet everybody to a standstill." As well he might.

Hiram tells us that Charlotte F. was a Thoroughbred, and "Mace had taught her to run so evenly and with such power of stroke, that she carried the old stallion along by the breeching at an enormous rate!"

Naturally, with two such national favorites involved, there was a tremendous crowd at the Fashion Course on June 21st, 1867, to see these two horses race for $2,000 a side, mile heats, three in five. There was equally tremendous disappointment, then, when the word came that the team was paying the $1250 forfeit and there would be no race! Charlotte F., it was made known, had injured herself and couldn't run. The bettors, who had been laying two to one on Dexter, as fast as they could, were especially voluble in their disappointment. Then another surprise: Ethan's party, after paying the forfeit, announced themselves willing, for only $500 a side, to race after all, using a pick-up runner, a "black gelding, captured in the war."

The bettors immediately were wilder than ever to lay two to one on Dexter. Ethan's chances were seen to be even slimmer, of course, trotting with a runner he wasn't acquainted with. Opinions on just how this all came about— whether Charlotte F. was really lame or not—differ somewhat, but one result of the fancy footwork that day was that John Morrissey, one of the team's "party," came out $40,000 ahead.

We have several eye-witness accounts of this race-of-the-titans, but the one I like best is contained in an appendix to Hiram's wonderful book, written by Charles Foster. (Hiram himself, unfortunately, died a few months before the race.)

In the first heat Dexter had the pole. They went off at an amazing speed, and at the quarter the double team led two lengths in 32 s. They maintained the rate, and went to the half-mile in 1 m.04 s., three lengths ahead. They were four lengths in the lead at the head of the stretch, and won by five lengths in 2 m. 15 s. A wonderful performance it was all round, but specially for Dexter, who trotted singly, and pulled his own vehicle and driver. He unquestionably beat 2 m. 17 s.

So great was the speed now that—the betting was even, it being thought that the team would give out before the end of three heats, while it was pretty well known that Dexter would 'stick.' Soon after they got the word in the second heat, the stallion broke. Dexter led a length on the turn, where he was trotting close to the outside. He took the pole before he reached the quarter, and went on with the lead to the half-mile, where his time was 1 m.06 s. But now the runner and the trotter had got to his wheel, having come through the straight work of the back stretch at a very high rate of speed. The pace was so hot that Ethan broke on the Flushing turn; but, when he caught, the runner whirled him along at such a rate that they overhauled Dexter, and beat him by three lengths in 2 m. 16 s. Dexter must have trotted this heat in 2 m. 17 s. or 2 m. 17,1/4 s.: and it affords the most notable example of consistency and courage that ever was seen; for, after he had trotted the first half-mile in the amazing time of 1 m. 06 s., and had kept the lead for three-quarters of a mile, he never left his feet when the team, like a storm, came rushing by, but trotted out to the end in 2 m. 17 s., or thereabouts. The team won the third heat in 2 m. 19 s.

The trotting of Dexter in this race settled three things in the minds of thoughtful and reasonable people: first, that, high as his powers had been estimated, they had been underrated; second, that no trotter going on equal terms with him had any chance to beat him; third, that a race between a trotter in single harness and another trotter in double harness with a running-mate, was no fair match. The conclusion was, that the running-horse beat Dexter.

But Dexter, who had been driven by Budd Doble since Hiram turned the gelding over to him in 1866, now went on to challenge the greatest adversary of all—time—and to win. In 1867, he beat Flora Temple's best mile of 2:19,3/4 by trotting one, on a half-mile track, in 2:19 flat, in the second heat of three. Then, as Mr. Foster went on to report:

....on the fourteenth of August, at Buffalo, Dexter was engaged by Doble to beat his own time on the Riverside Park at Boston. The famous little horse was brought out and warmed up. Doble then intimated to the judges that he should drive one round as preparatory. The horse went in... 2 m. 21,1/2 s. This was a great deal faster than Doble had intended to drive him, and indeed, most of the people thought that it was a real effort and failure. After being scraped and cooled out, Dexter was again harnessed and brought on the course at four o'clock. With him there came Ben Mace and the thoroughbred mare Charlotte F. ...She was under saddle, Mace riding; and it was his office to lay at Dexter's quarters, to keep up his emulation and his determination to conquer. A little jog or two, and then the trotter in harness, and the runner under saddle, went up to the stretch, and came along for the word. As Dexter was seen to be going very square and well, it was given. The pace was fast. He trotted the first quarter in 33,1/4 s., made the half-mile in 1 m. 07 s., and came home in 2 m. 17,1/4 s., in good wind, and with a stroke of commanding power.

Budd Doble wasn't noticeably pretty, either, but he trained and drove such cracks as Dexter and Goldsmith Maid, and was immortalized in Oliver Wendell Holmes's popular narrative poem, How the Old Horse Won the Bet.

This performance capped the climax of his fame, so far as trotting in public races is concerned.... My own opinion is, that Dexter can now go in less than 2 m. 20 s. any day and every day that he may be called upon to do so when he is fit to trot and the course is good. If that is correct, his regular rate is such that he must be capable of an effort so enormous, that he may, and probably will, far surpass his feat at Buffalo, and again make 'limping Time toil after him in vain.'

It is a shame that this great horse was gelded, but Dexter, unlike docile old Ethan Allen, was not noted for his good temper. His driver in later years, Budd Doble, wrote of him, however, that he "was not nearly as bad as he pretended to be. It is true that if a person went into his stall he would run at them and if they retreated he would follow them, although I do not think even then he would have injured anybody.... He was certainly not a pleasant-tempered horse, but I should not class him as a vicious animal." Hiram Woodruff also defended Dexter's disposition, but nonetheless he had a reputation for being cranky, and the fact that he was gelded tends to substantiate this.

Budd Doble's results with difficult Dexter were not a fluke. He was a great trainer and driver, and soon after this he became more famous then ever—as the driver of the "Queen of the Trotting Turf," Goldsmith Maid.

9
GEORGE WILKES

But with Dexter and Goldsmith Maid one is into the second half of the 1800s, and before "following the races" any further it is best to take a look at the sires and dams that were producing these ever-faster race horses. Not all of them were Hambletonians yet, of course, although many of them were descendants of Messenger (as Hambletonian was), and it wouldn't be long before most of the good trotters in the country *would* carry Hambletonian's blood. After all, Hambletonian got over 1300 foals over the years, most of them very fast, and horse breeders are not slow to recognize a good thing when they see it. However, stubbornness and prejudice did at times interfere with good judgment.

The first of Hambletonian's ungelded sons to received wide attention was the seal-brown stallion George Wilkes, named in honor of the editor of *The Spirit of the Times*, the most widely-read publication in America. George Wilkes the horse was foaled in 1856, two years before Dexter, in Newburgh, New York. His dam's name was Dolly Spanker (after a character in a popular play) and she was owned by a New Yorker, Judge Harry Felter. Both her pedigree and history have undergone several revisions, the most recently accepted being that her breeding was, alas, completely unknown. She was a brown mare, or brown-roan, small, very pretty, and up to doing a 3:00 clip, untrained and undeveloped for speed. She appears to have been, when almost six-years-old, bought from a cattleman by James Gilbert for $75, tack included, somewhere on the road between Erie and Meadville in westernmost Pennsylvania. Later, we find her being purchased by Judge Felter from "a circus man." From such peculiar beginnings came George Wilkes, the most influential of all Hambletonian's many influential sons.

Poor Dolly Spanker died from the effort of producing her seal-brown colt, and Judge Felter's "womenfolk" tenderly raised the orphan on, it is solemnly reported, a rather heady-sounding mixture of cow's milk, sugar, and Jamaica rum. Whether because of or in spite of this alcoholic formula, the tiny, weak orphan soon picked up considerably. So much so that when he was four years old "Bill" Simmons paid $4,000 for him, and *The Spirit of the Times* in 1862 described the then-six-year-old stallion this way:

> He is about 15.1 but all horse . . . His traveling gear is just what it should be — muscular shoulders, long strong arms, flat legs, splendid quarters, great length from hip to hock, and very fine back sinews. He stands higher behind than he does forward, a formation we like. . . . his coat is fine and glows like the rich dark tints of polished rosewood. . . . His temper is kind. We had the pleasure of seeing him at his work, and unless we are greatly mistaken he will make an amazingly good one. He has a long and easy way of going, striking out well behind and tucking his haunches well under him.

Charles Foster saw him trot, too, and remarked that, "his hind leg when straightened out in action as he went at his best pace reminded me of that of a duck swimming." This casual comment led to George Wilkes and many of his brood being called "duck gaited," or, meaning the same thing, "Wilkes gaited." It sounds awkward, but it didn't seem to slow any of them up.

The racing career of George Wilkes is interesting in that it points out something we probably should keep in mind. In those days — in fact, during the rest of the century — races were classified by time records. One race might be held for horses with time records slower than 2:35, for instance, a system meant to keep the competition fairly even and, of course, to give slower horses a chance to win once in a while. Once a horse made a better "mark" for himself, he was put into a better class of horses and made to work harder to win, with less chance of doing so. Therefore many drivers and trainers became well-known as "manipulators." By laying up their horses, and never letting them go faster than a desired rate of speed, they could keep winning races against much slower horses almost indefinitely. This, naturally, was very remunerative. And since it was difficult to prove that a horse wasn't going all out, there was very little that could be done about it.

But this whole business caused a great furor now and then, not to mention actual riots when bettors had reason to think that the horse they had backed had been pulled. A judge's lot was not a happy one in those days. The confusion was compounded by a different kind of laying up, one that was commonly used in order not to lose the race, but to win it. In a race of up to five heats a driver might well lay his horse up a heat or two just to save it, to win the race in later heats when the other horses had tired. This seemed perfectly fair and reasonable to the drivers, but not always to the bettors, who often bet on each heat as it came up. So this practice, too, while acted upon with honorable intentions in the long run, gave rise to riots, judges' stands being torn down, and drivers being thrown bodily off the grounds. In some ways harness racing was a much more colorful sport then.

At any rate, George Wilkes was "manipulated" by one driver after another throughout his entire career, it seems certain. The one driver he had who was *not* a manipulator was Hiram Woodruff, and he didn't last long with the owners. So while as a mere youngster of six George Wilkes beat the thirteen-year-old Ethan Allen, and subsequently won 56 heats in 2:30 or better (one in 2:24), we don't really know how fast he could have trotted. Many years later it was admitted, however, that his original trainer had timed him two successive miles in 2:19,1/4, 2:18,1/4 — before he had even developed his real speed.

He had been allowed to go fast enough to prove his worth, though, and long and hard enough to prove his "bottom." In twelve campaigns he had gone over 200 heats over all sorts of tracks, under saddle, in harness (sulky) and to wagon, during most of these campaigns also doing stud duty. He had earned his retirement, and then some. Moreover, he retired completely sound, after all this.

It would have been no surprise, then, had his instant popularity as a sire been assured. But it wasn't. Because George Wilkes had also earned a reputation as a quitter. At times he would drop almost to a standstill. One reason put forth for this was a two-mile trial in which he was pushed much too fast for his condition at the time. At least, it was right after this trial that he began his sulking. Also, he was a very high-tempered horse, and as so many such horses have, he resented the brutal whipping then common with most drivers, and perhaps he merely "got even" the only way he knew how. Whatever the causes may have been, it was obviously not a quality inherent in him, as his descendants were not known as quitters.

But by retirement age, George Wilkes's "quitter" label made him "almost friendless in the North." An added reason for this reputation was his manager's insistence on running him into the ground, so that after twelve grueling campaigns the public tended to forget his more glorious youth and to remember the old worn-out campaigner he was at the end, being obstinately put against younger, faster horses. All in all, George Wilkes was not treated fairly in any respect.

Fortunately there was one Northern horseman who remembered George Wilkes from his better days, and had faith in him as a sire. William H. Wilson then did two things that ultimately resulted in George Wilkes and his get bringing Kentucky into the trotting picture in a big way. He married a girl from Kentucky; and he leased George Wilkes from the Simmons Brothers. Then he took both his new associates to a farm he rented near Lexington, known as Ash Grove.

Kentucky did not welcome the new stallion with open arms. They didn't particularly care that much for trotters yet, and they didn't care at all for quitters. And they liked their horses beautiful, like their Thoroughbreds and Saddle Horses. The Blue Grass horsemen sneeringly referred to the 17-year-old son of Hambletonian as "Bill Simmons' baked-up pony" and proceeded to ignore him in droves. What few trotting sires there were in Kentucky by this time (1873) were magnificent ones, like Mambrino Patchen, Mambrino King ("the handsomest horse in the world") and others of similar standing. The seal-brown orphan had, as Hervey remarked, "a hard row to hoe."

But he had in Wilson an indefatigable ally, who went to work with a will. The first thing he did was to convince the Kentuckians that they needed to organize, and this resulted, in 1874, in the Kentucky Trotting Horse Breeders' Association. Wilson, as it happened, was its president.

Then he set to work making George Wilkes a respectable sire. He *knew* that his horse's bloodlines were great, and in order to prove it he beat the bushes for mares. If the owner of a good mare had no money, he bred her on shares; he gave discounts; he leased mares he could get no other way; and against great indifference, if not active opposition, he managed to bring 82 mares to George Wilkes in 1874. This was a brilliant success, hard won, but it proved to be his downfall. For when Simmons learned how well George Wilkes was doing down in Kentucky, he decided not to renew Wilson's one-year lease. Instead, he moved down there himself, bought Ash Grove, and took over, setting up his own breeding establishment. William Wilson, it seems, was to be treated fully as unfairly as George Wilkes had always been.

George Wilkes's splendid blood, now that it was allowed to prove itself, resulted, in the nine years when he was seventeen to twenty-six-years old, in about 300 "performers" (horses that did 2:30 or better) and "producers" (dams of performers). And, after the first crop or two began to show their stuff, "the Wilkes boom" was on. After such a miserable beginning, George Wilkes became "the progenitor of the fastest and most successful branch of the Hambletonian family," and now his blood is nearly as all-pervading in the Standardbred as is his illustrious sire's. Today his most distinguished remaining tail-male line is that of his son William L., through Axworthy. Perhaps his most famous descendant was the long-time world champion trotter, Greyhound. George Wilkes also sired many pacing stars, and as well contributed mightily to the then-developing Tennessee Walking Horse, since his descendant, Allan F. 1, was the foundation sire of that breed.

It is a strange story, and in many ways an unhappy one, but a story with a most satisfying ending. George Wilkes was but one of the many, many horses throughout history who deserved better treatment than they received, but at least he had one good friend for one year who believed in him, and that is all he needed.

10
MORE HAMBLETONIANS

Of all the fine sons of Hambletonian with the exception of George Wilkes, three others stand out as having founded "sub-families" of their own of great and lasting importance. These were Alexander's Abdallah (Abdallah 15 in the Registry), Electioneer, and Happy Medium.

Alexander's Abdallah's story is short and tragic. A "rich, solid bay" with one white foot, he was foaled in Orange County in 1852. His dam was Katy Darling, one of those fast road mares that were being bred to Hambletonian in such great numbers. Her owner, Mr. Sutton, had picked her up cheaply at a roadhouse. She was "standing on three legs" at the time, but he decided to breed her on the strength of her good conformation and her former trotting style.

Her foal was so handsome, and so noted for his infant trotting action — Wallace referred to the colt's "persistency in cavorting around at that gait" — that he was soon purchased from his breeder for $500 by Major Edsall and was named Edsall's Hambletonian. After a few local races and some stud duty in Orange County, Edsall sold him to two Kentuckians for $3,000, a most astonishing price at that time, but one that shows clearly how popular Hambletonian's get already were, even though the "patriarch" was then only three years old!

He was taken to Kentucky in 1858, and was so successful that in 1863 he was purchased by R. A. Alexander for his famous Woodburn Farm, already noted for its Thoroughbreds, especially the renowned stallion Lexington. He was then renamed Alexander's Abdallah.

However, the Civil War raged ever closer, and the Kentucky horse farms were a prime target of the Confederate raiders, including the notorious Marion. At night on February 2, 1865, Marion's guerillas attacked Woodburn and made off with many horses — among them Abdallah and a well-known young trotter named Bay Chief. Wallace described the ensuing nightmare:

> Marion mounted Bay Chief and, crossing the Kentucky River, the band encamped . . . twelve miles from Woodburn. Here the next morning the Federal

calvary were sent in pursuit after the raid, came up with the raiders, and after a sharp fight routed them. Marion, on Bay Chief, was a conspicuous mark for Federal bullets during the skirmish. Early in the fray Bay Chief was shot through the muzzle, through both thighs, and one hock. In this condition he carried his rider two miles in retreat, when the horse was so weakened by loss of blood that a Federal calvalryman overtook them. . . . Bay Chief died about ten days later, despite all efforts made to save him. Meanwhile, Alexander's Abdallah had been found, safe and sound, by a Federal soldier in Mr. Bush's stable. The soldier refused to give him up to Mr. Alexander's men, and declared he would send him North and keep him until he got a large reward for his return. The horse was barefooted and in no condition for hard usage. And so they rode him off, and after going some forty or fifty miles [and after being ridden hot through a cold river] he gave out, and they turned him loose on the road. He was found next day in a pitiable condition by the roadside, and brought back as far as Lawrenceburg on his way home, where he was taken with pneumonia and died a few days later.

Just how great a loss this was to the trotting breed was not realized until long after —until in fact Goldsmith Maid [his daughter] had conquered all before her . . . and until his two great sons, Almont and Belmont, rose to pre-eminent places in the list of great sires.

Alexander's Abdallah was only thirteen-years-old when he died for such an abominable reason, and had served far too few years in the stud. In fact, his own sire, Hambletonian, outlived Abdallah a full eleven years. Alexander's Abdallah, like George Wilkes, also produced many descendants who were fast pacers, as well as many trotters. This is probably due to the fact that there was so much pacing blood in the mares of Kentucky, Tennessee, and Indiana at that time, although we should remember that pacing was still not considered a respectable harness gait, but only valued for its necessary contribution to the saddle-gaited horses.

Almont and Belmont, Woodburn's premier sires for many years, were both sired by Alexander's Abdallah and both out of daughters of Mambrino Chief. They were also both foaled in 1864 and, through their dams' lines, possessed a rich inheritance of pacing blood, and both stallions were fast-trotting bays. Between them, they carried on the line most successfully, siring both trotters and pacers.

Happy Medium, the second son of Hambletonian to be considered here, had a much better known dam than Alexander's Abdallah's. She was the famous race mare, Princess, a great campaigner and a chief rival of Flora Temple. Happy Medium was foaled in the very middle of the Civil War, in 1863, but fortunately in Suffern County, New York, out of harm's way. According to Hervey, Happy Medium's is the dominant surviving male Hambletonian line. He was a good-looking bay horse, 15.2 hands, with a nice head carriage and an exceptionally pure trotting gait. He was first owned by Princess' owner, George Alley, but Alley sold him as a weanling to Ransom Galloway. After some "amateurish training" by Galloway, and three races, which he won, he was sold in 1871 to Robert Steel, who had established a new farm near Philadelphia with Budd Doble as his advisor. Steel created no small sensation by this purchase, as he paid $25,000 for Happy Medium, a price until then unheard of for a trotting stallion. He kept him for eight years, at a $100 stud fee, and then, after collecting some $40,000 in this manner, sold him to Fairlawn Farm at Lexington, Kentucky, where Happy Medium died at twenty-five, in 1888.

All was not as rosy in Happy Medium's career as it may seem, however. Once again a prejudicial attitude sprang up that proved to be an undeserved obstacle. At first, he was well received. "The Happy Mediums all trot," they said. His get were much in demand, being easy to train, good-gaited, and handsome. Moreover, they had early speed — they didn't require several years of training to settle down and trot fast. But horsemen of those days weren't quite ready for such naturally gaited horses, or for such early speed. Even though the first crops were setting records and winning races, in a few years the attitude developed that the Happy Mediums were "soft-hearted" and couldn't stand the gaff, and this naturally affected the stallion's reputation. As Hervey pointed out, however, this was almost surely a misunderstanding.

Because so many of the old-time trotters were really repressed, "reformed" pacers, most trainers expected to have to work a horse half to death just to develop and keep a trot, let alone to get up any speed at that gait. But the Happy Mediums were *natural* trotters. They simply didn't need all that endless work to be prepared to race, and it tended to wear them down.

Other factors working against Happy Medium's founding a family were the undeniable facts that his sons were all sold to other states; that his mares were mostly "short-bred" (lacking long, known pedigrees); and that Kentucky, after the talk of his get's supposed softness, rejected him. All of this counted against him, and yet, in spite of so much adversity, his line still managed not only to survive but to dominate. One of his daughters was Nancy Hanks, who lowered the world's trotting record to 2:04 in 1892, but by that time Happy Medium was dead. And one of his grand-daughters was Lou Dillon, the first two-minute mare in history, while his grandson, Peter the Great, was an unparallelled Standardbred sire. It is interesting to note that Happy Medium, of all Hambletonian's sons, was the most inbred to Messenger.

As a sire of early speed, though, Electioneer, the third son of Hambletonian to be discussed here, surpassed all others to date and helped to revolutionize harness racing in this respect. He was also outstanding for being able to produce natural-gaited trotters from running-bred mares, something no other stallion had ever truly succeeded in doing.

In 1875, Leland Stanford, the ex-governor of California, established a breeding farm in that state which he called Palo Alto. To upgrade his trotting-bred stock (he also had Thoroughbreds), in 1876 he made a trip back East to select and purchase the best he could find there. This news spread swiftly, as it will in horsey circles, especially since it was known that "money was no object." Which stallion would he choose, from which breeder, and what would be the price?

By that time Hambletonian's line was fully established as the best, and Orange County as the trotting horse center of the world, and Charles Backman's Stony Ford Farm possessed the best collection of sons of Hambletonian in Orange County. Therefore Governor Stanford arrived at Stony Ford, accompanied by a clutch of advisors and experts and general, all-purpose busy-bodies, among them both Wallace and Busbey. The premier sire at Stony Ford in those days was Messenger Duroc, an aged horse with fine blood and a good reputation as a sire, and the consensus (before he even arrived) was that Governor Stanford should be persuaded to buy Messenger Duroc, especially since Backman entertained visions of getting over $50,000 for him.

When the time came, and the dozen or so sons of Hambletonian were trotted out and looked over, appropriate remarks were made by the advisors. Stanford, however, didn't let on which, if any, he liked. He bought several mares at staggering prices, and then they all trooped into the house for dinner. Afterward, having said little all day, Stanford asked a very surprised Backman what the price might be on the eight-year-old stallion called Electioneer, a horse he had seemed hardly to notice earlier. The hangers-on were all stunned, having supposed they had done their work well in selling Stanford on Messenger Duroc. Perhaps they didn't think Stanford was even serious, but on Christmas Eve, 1876, when the band of brood mares arrived at Palo Alto, Electioneer was with them, having changed hands for $12,500.

Electioneer's dam was Green Mountain Maid, one day to be known as "the great mother of trotters." She was a 15-hand brown mare, sired by Harry Clay out of Shanghai Mary, "a bloodlike mare of nervous temperament." Shanghai Mary was once traded for a pair of steers worth about $40 plus $10 in cash. Her value gradually rose until Hiram Woodruff bought her for a client for $1,400, whereupon she "didn't train on." This was still a small price for the dam of such a mare as Green Mountain Maid. As a race horse the Maid was worthless, as she was so "wild and uncontrollable" that her training was abandoned after one hapless attempt. This was unfortunate because, Busbey tells us, "In her young days Green Mountain Maid led the brood mares at Stony Ford at a trot; she could go no other gait."

But as a brood mare, she was to be unequaled. When she died in 1888, Backman marked her grave by a granite monument engraved with her name, a list of her eleven children and their time-records, and ending with the touching line, "This stone was erected A.D. 1889, by Charles Backman, on the spot dedicated to her worth and honored by her dust."

So Governor Stanford, in his quiet way, had chosen well. His new stallion Electioneer was a dark bay, sometimes called brown, and was 15.2 at the withers and 15.3 at the quarters. He was stocky, rather short in the leg, and very compact, and had never been raced or even trained much. His success in California touched off two sorts of revolutions. One, with his get attaining such amazingly early speed, Stanford invented a totally new way to train trotters. Instead of waiting until they were four or five and bringing them along slowly for the next few years, he began to train *weanlings*. Not in harness, of course, but in a small, carefully fenced-in track, where the foals were kept freely moving, until they dropped into a trot and stayed there. Soon two-year-olds would actually be in harness and racing in California, and most of these "racing babies" would be Electioneer's.

The second revolution came about as a result of Electioneer's unusual gait. Until this time the best trotters had always been supposed to be the "open-gaited" ones, or as they were sometimes called, "passing-gaited." This meant that when trotting fast, their hind feet passed by their front ones on the outside. Horses that didn't trot that way naturally were taught to, if possible, which was called "opening them up." This open-gaitedness was a direct inheritance from Messenger and Hambletonian, and highly valued. To say that one could "roll a barrel between his hind feet" was a compliment. Horses so spraddle-gaited did of course have immense reach, but the gait was hard to control and probably contributed to the fact that these trotters broke so often when pressed hard. George Wilkes, with his "duck paddle," was extremely open-gaited. Electioneer's get, on the contrary, were usually "line-gaited," as well as early starters. Their hind feet simply tracked on a line with their front feet, rather than passing them. This meant a shorter stride, and it was accompanied by unusually high action in front, so horsemen for a time thought that therefore the Electioneers wouldn't be able to trot fast. They did it all wrong! Horsemen were eventually disabused of that supposition, but even so there arose against the Electioneers a terrible hostility.

This was yet another of those bigoted, political, short-sighted faction fights, and one that did a great disservice to the breed. It helps to understand this if you keep in mind that in Kentucky by this time "the Wilkes boom" was in full sway. Kentucky was also beginning to gain considerable influence in trotting-bred circles, having finally accepted trotters as being worth breeding. Therefore there were many people who owned Wilkes-bred stock and who wanted to get the best prices for them, and some of these were prominent people. When the Electioneers seemed to threaten them, their reaction was to "propagandize" heatedly against them. Electioneer's get were called quitters.

But, as before, all this was aided by the fact that many horsemen truly believed that they *were* quitters, when really they were, like Happy Medium's, simply so naturally gaited and had so much early speed that the old-time horsemen didn't really know how to cope with them. They weren't ready for the "revolution" toward early speed and short races, and they didn't understand what was happening. In the old days, the split-heat races had become popular primarily because the old-time stock *was* so hard to train and to keep from breaking gait. With three or more heats, each horse had a better chance to complete at least one or two of them without breaking disastrously, and when one reads descriptions of those old races one's greatest impression is often of horses breaking, jumping and hopping constantly. One of a trainer's principal objects was, as a matter of fact, to teach a trotter how to "catch" quickly — to get back to his gait after a break without losing too much ground. Then, as now, of course, a horse that broke, or "left his feet," had by the rules to be pulled until he settled back to his trot.

These two things — the Wilkes faction's "propagandizing" and the utter novelty of the Electioneers' early speed and natural ability, combined to cause this very valuable blood to be sadly neglected. Just how valuable it was is indicated by the fact that previously the world's record for two-year-old trotters had been 2:31. The first crop of Electioneers in California lowered that to an incredible 2:10,3/4!

Fortunately Electioneer's owner had his own good mares to breed to him, and other mare owners weren't 100% against him. And just as Goldsmith Maid one day vindicated her sire Alexander's Abdallah, in 1903 a great-granddaughter of Happy Medium and daughter of Electioneer, named Lou Dillon, vindicated both those ancestors with the long-awaited two-minute mile. The Standardbred breed improved with amazing rapidity, but we can't help wondering — what if, instead of doing battle so bitterly, the Wilkes faction had welcomed Electioneer blood and crossed it extensively with that of George Wilkes?

There were, of course, more than three important sons of Hambletonian. In fact, there were a great many of them — Strathmore, the only one we know of who was a pacer, and Jay Gould among them — but the three "sub-families" inspected here have proved to be of the most enduring importance.

11
THE CHIEFS AND THE PILOTS

Mambrino Chief was not descended from Hambletonian. But he and Hambletonian shared the same grandsire in Mambrino and therefore the same great-grandsire in Messenger:

Mambrino Chief by Mambrino Paymaster by Mambrino by Messenger. Hambletonian by Abdallah by Mambrino by Messenger.

Mambrino Chief was the first really successful trotting sire to arrive in Kentucky. True, Abdallah, Hambletonian's sire, had spent one season there fourteen years before, but the Blue Grass horsemen had enthusiastically rejected him. Another son of Mambrino named Commodore had accompanied Old Abdallah, and was widely used in Kentucky, but for some reason he got no good trotters. So Mambrino Chief's arrival there in 1854 was a new start, and his line proved to be the most influential of those not descended from Hambletonian.

He was foaled in 1844, five years before Hambletonian, in Dutchess County, New York, and as noted, was sired by Mambrino Paymaster. This Paymaster was a huge horse at 16.2, coarse, and noted as a speed sire. Chief's dam, according to Wallace, was "a large, coarse mare that was brought from the West in a drove ("the West" in those days usually meant western New York or Pennsylvania) and absolutely nothing was known of her blood." It was known, though, that she was a grand road mare and farm worker, producing at least three fast-trotting foals before, still going strong, she died at the age of thirty from the effects of an accident.

From this description of his parents, then, it seems reasonable that Mambrino Chief himself was huge and coarse. Considering the Kentuckians' predilection for beautiful horses, however, it does come as a surprise that "the Chief" was accepted there. But he was accepted, and for a very good and very important reason.

Until Mambrino Chief's arrival, harness racing was so absolutely frowned on in Kentucky that trotters were actually barred from using Kentucky race tracks. Kentuckians considered themselves aristocrats and, as such, would only countenance running races and the breeding of Thoroughbreds for racing. For saddle and harness they were in the process of developing—from Thoroughbred, Morgan and pacing stock—their already famous Saddlebreds, which were fine-boned horses of tremendous beauty, stamina, and style. Anyone so bold as to attempt to breed trotting-bred horses or race them was

Mambrino Chief was the first successful trotting horse sire in Kentucky.

quickly "drummed out of the lodge." One man was even asked to leave his church because he wanted to race trotters. This is in startling and humorous contrast to the Northeastern states, where running races were "immoral" and often even illegal. But prominent clergymen were defending their right to drive trotters that could "go better than 2:40," engaging in brushes on the way to preach their sermons, and attending trotting races with the solemn explanation that since a horse can gallop faster than it can trot, obviously a trotting horse wasn't going as fast as it could, and therefore couldn't be said to be really "racing!"

Many of the Kentuckians came from the Southern coastal states, where Thoroughbreds were meant for racing and saddle-gaited horses for riding and driving. Trotters were for Yankees, which helps explain this early, extreme distaste for trotters. But then an unusual thing happened. James B. Clay, the son of Henry Clay, who was the absolute ideal of all Kentuckians, dismayed one and all by suddenly deciding to raise trotters and race them. This put the entire state in a froth. The very idea of "old Henry's" famous Thoroughbred farm Ashland being turned over to trotters was appalling. Blue Grass horsemen couldn't have been more upset if Clay had announced he was establishing a pig farm.

But such was James Clay's standing, wealth, and political and social clout that everyone else simply had to accept his derangement. It is doubtful if, at that time, any other single person in Kentucky could have succeeded in such an undertaking. The great prejudice against trotters didn't disappear overnight, but from then on it began to lose its power.

In February, 1854, Mambrino Chief arrived at Ashland, near Lexington, having been purchased by Clay and having been ridden down from Dutchess County by Clay's agent. On that day Kentucky began its swift overtaking of New York as the premier breeding site of trotters and pacers, as well as Thoroughbreds and Saddle Horses. The Chief was then already ten years old, but had sired no remarkable horses in New York. Once he reached the Blue Grass, however, and had access to the area's many fine, well-bred mares, he seemed to have found the kind of stock with which his blood crossed best.

Mambrino Chief, in spite of his coarseness, was immediately in business, having 80 mares brought to him his first year at $25 each. He only stayed at Ashland for three years, though, and in 1857 Clay sold him to Gray and Jones for $5,020. The Civil War seemed inevitable by then and Clay had decided he'd better liquidate some of his stock. In fact, when war did break out in 1861 and Kentucky remained loyal to the Union, Clay, who was an outspoken Secessionist, was indicted for treason and only just managed to escape to Canada.

On being sold in 1857, the Chief was moved to neighboring Woodford County and enjoyed tremendous continued success until his death in 1862, at eighteen-years-old.

In appearance Mambrino Chief was a blackish brown, 16 hands high, with the coarseness he was famous for, topped off by a huge, heavy head, which he generously passed on to many of his descendants. Another feature he often passed along was a strange one—a hind leg that was *gray*.

However, and oddly enough, Mambrino Chief—when bred to some of Kentucky's lovely, fine-boned, saddle-type mares—sired some beautiful horses. One of the most handsome was Mambrino Patchen, a trotting horse sire and also a very important sire in the Saddle Horse Registry. The oddest thing about this is that the Saddle Horse breeders, notably General Castleman, could not and would not believe that "their" horse Mambrino Patchen could possibly have been sired by a coarse, huge-headed monster like

Mambrino King was known as "the most beautiful horse in the world." His grandsire was Mambrino Chief, according to the Standardbred records, or Gaines's Denmark, according to the American Saddle Horse registry.

Mambrino Chief, and they decided—and eventually made it official—that Patchen's real father must have been the Saddle Horses' beautiful Thoroughbred foundation sire, Denmark. So Mambrino Patchen has the distinction of not only being an important sire in the registries of two different breeds (which is not too uncommon) but also of having two different, "official," sires.

The Saddle Horse people based their opinion on the appearances of the horses, and on the fact that Denmark and Mambrino Chief were stabled together at the time of Mambrino Patchen's conception. However, they seem not to have noticed that Mambrino Patchen, while otherwise coal-black, had one gray hind leg, a feature often seen and remarked on in Mambrino Chief's get (and his descendants, even to this day), but certainly never seen in any of Denmark's progeny. How such a distinctive, noticeable, and talked-about feature could be overlooked is somewhat mystifying.

As a sire of what would one day be known as Standardbreds, however, there is no argument about Mambrino Patchen's importance, and in the Standardbred Registry he is a son of Mambrino Chief. He was not raced, his widely admired appearance and his bloodlines making him a popular sire from the outset. His full sister, though, Lady Thorn, became a most famous race mare. One of Patchen's sons, Mambrino King, was so outstandingly gorgeous that he was known as "the most beautiful horse in the world." He was a great show ring champion and a Saddle Horse sire, but he was also a trotting sire. Generally speaking, however, Mambrino Patchen's most vital contribution to the Standardbred was as a brood mare sire; his daughters soon becoming deservedly renowned for producing speed from a variety of stallions. The importance of a good brood mare sire is sometimes overlooked, but it should never be underestimated. It is of vast value to a breed to have a prepotent stallion capable of getting good colts out of all sorts of mares. But it is also a great boost to have him sire a flock of mares that seem to produce good foals from all sorts of stallions.

As a sire of race horses, Mambrino Patchen sired plenty of early speed, but few trotters that lasted to become track stars after they matured—perhaps at least partly because of improper handling. The fact that he is present in the pedigrees of so many present-day Standardbreds is due mostly, therefore, to his marvelous daughters.

Mambrino Chief's only important rival stallion in Kentucky in the trotting line was Pilot Jr., also foaled in 1844, right there in the Blue Grass State.

His sire, Pilot (or "Old Pacing Pilot"), was a black pacer with a mysterious beginning. He has always been called a Canadian pacer, and he probably was one, but nothing at all is known about his breeding. There is a story that as a young horse he once appeared in New Orleans "hitched to a peddler's cart." This, by the way, doesn't mean that he was a cart horse. It only means that at that time he was owned by what today would be called a hustler. Men with a foot-loose disposition would sometimes get themselves a pretty fast horse and simply set out to travel around the country with it. When they got to a new town, then, they could often make some pocket money by offering to race their "cart horse" with the local speedster, and, if theirs was fast enough, beating it. Once in a while they needed considerable speed just to get out of town ahead of the posse.

At any rate, in New Orleans, the "peddler" confided in a local sportsman, Major Dubois, and when, it is reported, he showed the Major a mile in 2:26, carrying a 165-pound man, the Major bought the black pacer for $1,000 "in sugar."

Then, Pilot being about six years old at that time, he was re-sold to a livery stable company at Louisville, where he was kept at stud until his death in about 1855. As might be expected, most of his get were pacers. After his trotting son, Pilot Jr., became famous, attempts were made to prove that Old Pilot trotted as well as paced, but Wallace insisted that he did not. Wallace was well-acquainted with a prominent neighboring horse breeder who knew the old horse well, and he told Wallace very firmly that "his master could not make him trot a step. On the occasion of a very deep fall of snow he was taken out to see whether that would not compel him to trot, and he went rolling and tumbling about with no more gait than a hobbled hog."

Pilot Jr., as we mentioned, was one of the few trotters his sire begot, and he was a good one. Foaled in 1844, he was trained and won some races, and eventually, when fourteen-years-old, was bought by R. A. Alexander for

Woodburn Farm. Woodburn had followed James Clay's lead by establishing a large "trotting division" along with its enormous Thoroughbred operation. Pilot Jr. was a gray, and figures prominently in modern-day pacing pedigrees, although, like Mambrino Patchen, principally through his daughters.

It should never be forgotten that Kentucky, Tennessee, and Indiana were more drastically and directly affected by the Civil War than was the more fortunate state of New York. The horse stock of the entire country was ravaged, of course, many of the most finely bred horses being lost to bullets and to the diseases that swept through the cavalry herds. But Orange and Dutchess County farms, and New England ones, were at least not raided by Confederates. Many of Mambrino Patchen's and Pilot Jr.'s progeny were lost during the war years, while on Long Island they were still enjoying a full racing schedule.

In spite of this violent attrition, and in spite of the slow, high-wheeled sulkies of the day, Pilot Jr. put eight performers on the 2:30 list, and, as Wallace put it, "His daughters are among the glories of the Trotting Register." Mambrino Patchen, for his part, got twenty-five performers. And these three stallions—Mambrino Chief, Mambrino Patchen and Pilot Jr.—put Kentucky in the trotting horse business in a big way, bringing that state to a position of eminence it has yet to relinquish.

12
STARS, BULLS AND CLAYS

While Hambletonian, Mambrino Chief and Pilot Jr. were the most influential early sires of the trotting and pacing horses of today, they were not the only ones, of course. At various times several other families were touted as their rivals, and although history would prove them to be indeed important it would also prove their failure as highly dominant factors over the long run. Their blood was necessary, however, and vital. Inbreeding is fine, and has produced many of our greatest horses (especially those inbred Messengers and inbred Hambletonians we keep running across)—but it does have its limits. No one horse can do it all.

The Star family gets its name from Seely's American Star 14, foaled in 1837 in New Jersey and bred by Judge Henry J. Berry. His dam's name was Sally Slouch! She was "said to be" sired by Henry, the famous running race horse. This was never proved, but the Star family *was* known to suffer from defective feet and legs, a "Henry" characteristic.

American Star's sire line is even less certain. Mr. Battell, the indefatigable Morgan horse researcher, claimed this horse's sire was a Morgan descendant, but that was never proved to anyone's satisfaction but his—which doesn't mean that it couldn't very well be true, even though American Star had absolutely no typical Morgan traits. As was seen earlier, Black Hawk "didn't talk like a Morgan," either, but the Morgan line tended to do that, when crossed on completely different types. The *advertised* sire of American Star 14 was Stockholm's American Star, a Thoroughbred son of Duroc, but Wallace showed that that advertisement was full of holes and therefore was automatically suspect. Nobody seems to have really known, even then, who this horse's father was, so it's highly unlikely that we'll ever know, now.

But the important thing is what kind of horses he himself sired. His typical get were "low-headed and long-gaited, with wide action behind"—those open-gaited trotters that were so highly valued. Nonetheless, American Star was not appreciated during his lifetime, and suffered hard usage by several owners until he died in 1861, never having earned more than $25 for a stud fee. And he died as he had lived. The twenty-four-year-old, over-worked horse was unhumanely turned out into a barren lot (in February!), where he died from starvation and exposure, apparently to no one's great regret.

But a few years later, this tragic scene was accompanied by the sudden realization that his daughters, when bred to Hambletonian, produced fantastic trotters, and these daughters were then sought after and considered very valuable. The result of one such cross, among many, was Dexter.

The story of the Clay family is more cheerful. It begins in 1820 when an iron-gray, 14.2-hand Barb stallion called Grand Bashaw was imported from Tripoli. When Pearl, a grand-daughter of Messenger, was bred to him she produced Young Bashaw. When he in turn was bred to "a trotting and pacing mare," the result in 1827 was Andrew Jackson, a handsome, fast-trotting black stallion 15.2 hands high, the first trotting stallion to do much on the tracks and become nationally known. (Until then, stallions were rarely raced.)

In 1837, Andrew Jackson became the sire of Henry Clay. His dam was Mr. George M. Patchen's "road-race mare," Lady Surrey, "a fast trotting mare," but one who had been converted to that gait from her natural pace. Henry Clay was also jet black and 15.2 hands high. Although Henry Clay was untrained and unraced, he enjoyed great popularity as a sire. And although he got few really fast trotters (only two sons made the 2:30 list), he did sire one that went on to make his name for him. The brown colt that would save Henry Clay from obscurity was foaled in 1843 out of a "fine road mare" named Jersey Kate, and was named Cassius M. Clay. He in turn also produced only one great horse, and that was the famous George M. Patchen.

Actually the Clay family is often called the Clay-Patchen family and well it might be. George M. Patchen was a bay stallion, a good 16 hands high and powerfully built. He was foaled the same year as Hambletonian (1849) and for quite a time the Patchens were serious rivals of the Hambletonians. His dam's name is lost now.

George M. Patchen had several owners. His turf career extended from 1855 to 1863, and his first race was against "no less a celebrity than Ethan Allen." Ethan Allen, then only seven years old to Patchen's six, reacted to his emerging rival by trouncing him—he distanced Patchen, in fact. Five years later, however, in 1860, the two met again in two matches a week apart, and both times Patchen won in straight heats, all under 2:30! This made Patchen the trotting stallion champion at eleven years old. The Clay-Patchen family, according to Wallace, faded from its brief glory to a minor family because of "its poverty in recognized trotting blood." But it made its mark on the breed while it lasted.

Blue Bull's story is the most mysterious of the lot. It really belongs to the pacers, and would be here so presented, except that during the period that the Blue Bulls took the country by storm pacers were still in disgrace. Therefore most of this stallion's progeny were forced to change to the trot. This, said Hervey, is why Blue Bull could put no fewer than 55 trotters on the 2:30 list; they were all, he contended, converted to that gait by the heavy shoes, toe weights, and other methods then in constant use for "reforming" pacers. This seems logical, as Blue Bull was definitely a pacer, his sons (after having raced as trotters) sired pacers, and his daughters produced pacers. His influence, as it was, was great. If he had been born fifty years later, it would have been tremendous.

Blue Bull's breeding, after all the literature produced in the effort to establish it is read, comes out finally as "unknown." It seems to have had something to do with some dun and blue (blue roan) stallions that were possibly of part draft blood and all named something-or-other-Bull, and some even more mysterious mares. Great effort went into the search for Blue Bull's pedigree, as a great many people had money invested in his progeny. Unfortunately, there was so much invested that, Wallace claimed, this search was rendered almost hopeless from the start. As he put it,

> Whenever a horse of unknown breeding, in any one of three or four states, began to show some speed, his owner at once called him a Blue Bull, and if he went fast enough to enter the 2:30 list, he was at once credited to Blue Bull by his friends, and they were all ready to fight for it. If the books of Blue Bull's services did not show that the dam of the 'unknown' had ever been within a hundred miles of that horse, it was all the worse for the books. With a large number of men financially interested in Blue Bull stock, ready to claim everything in sight and anxiously looking for something more to appear, it became a most laborious task to keep this class of frauds out of the records.

This stallion is so "mysterious," in fact, that while Hervey gives his foaling date as 1855, Wallace gives us 1858. They agree that he died in 1880.

He was foaled in Indiana (that much seems sure), and except for a few breeding-circuit journeys into Kentucky and perhaps Ohio, he stayed in that state all his life. For a time Indiana held sway as the center of trotting-horse breeding, with many big stud farms there. Blue Bull was neither a bull nor blue—he was a chestnut horse, his name apparently coming from a blue roan known as Merring's Blue Bull that was purported by many to have been his grand-sire. He wasn't very "bullish" in size, either, being barely over 15 hands, but he was strongly built, with a high, "breedy" head, a long neck, and fine legs. He was also a very fast pacer, who could "not trot a step himself."

He first received attention in 1871 (when he was either thirteen or sixteen years old) when the Long Island and vicinity race tracks began to be invaded by "hoosier" horses, an astonishing number of which could trot in 2:30 or better, and most of them by (or said to be by) a hitherto unnoticed stallion called Blue Bull, from Indiana, of all places. It was a well-known feature of these western speedsters that their pedigrees were, in many cases, a bit muddy, but another more striking feature was the way they kept winning.

In 1884 Blue Bull's enduring fame was assured, for that year he became the only sire to beget more 2:30 horses than Hambletonian himself—40, to Hambletonian's 38. This supremacy lasted only two years, but during his lifetime Blue Bull sired 49 sons who would in turn sire 2:30 performers, and 117 daughters who would produce them. This was a remarkable record, especially considering the high-wheeled sulkies and slow tracks of the times, and it earned Blue Bull much renown. Today, few fast trotters trace back to him. But, with pacers supreme now, this is more than compensated for by his prevalence in many of our best pacing strains.

There were other, more "minor" families and sub-families, that comprised this complex web of the early Standardbred. It is even more complex than the early Thoroughbred, because trotters and pacers were the horses of the people. Thoroughbreds were more strictly race horses, most often owned and bred by "aristocrats" only for racing, and as such they were more of "a breed apart." As we have seen, many of the greatest trotting-bred horses sprang from humble, often unknown, origins. If a man owned a fast harness mare, the fact that she was otherwise undistinguished—in appearance or by blood—didn't keep him from breeding her to a good trotting stallion, and often the results were splendid. The breed developed on its merits, in other words.

Bloodlines were certainly not disregarded, especially later on, but a mare who was, in herself, a good road mare, was not barred from breeding because she had a short or unknown pedigree. If she could get down the road in a hurry and had plenty of bottom and spirit to boot, she was worth breeding. This is a condition that now gives historians the hives, but without doubt it also was greatly responsible for giving the Standardbred its speed, toughness and durability. The eventual coming of the Register, and its rules for entry, would clarify matters a great deal, but even then—as there is now—there was and is a "loophole" allowing for the entry of a horse, regardless of breeding, that *merits* it by its proven performance. This is unusual, and typically American, in approach and attitude.

But with the appearance and recognition of certain foundation sires and more or less definite families, certain patterns of breeding were emerging. Pedigrees began to mean more, and breeders began to keep better records. "Mr. Seely's crippled brown mare" was no longer a good enough identification for a well-bred horse's mother. She had to at least have a *name*, and preferably also a father and mother of her own. Breeding associations began to be formed—like the one Mr. Wilson formed in Kentucky—for the purposes of keeping records, investigating pedigrees, and deciding on goals for breeders.

Wallace, in spite of all the things that have been said against him for his arrogance and pugnacity and his "obsession" about the supreme power of pacing blood, began the first registration of trotters. At first, it was just some trotting horse pedigrees added on to his original work, a Thoroughbred Stud Book. Then, after some setbacks, not the least of which was the way he aroused the animosity of the Kentucky breeders by sarcastically rejecting their idea for a "standard," in his magazine "Wallace's Monthly," he established a Registry of his own by painstakingly tracking down hundreds of pedigrees. He compiled his list with only "a general conception of the families that had produced trotters and those that had not." He added, "I had no rule by which I could decide what to admit and what to reject, except that all actual performers of reputable speed must be admitted." (On their merit.)

Wallace took a great interest in the formation of the National Association of Trotting Horse Breeders, and "upon the organization of the association, its character was so entirely acceptable to me that I did not hesitate to place in its hands the supervisory control of the registration of pedigrees for the 'Trotting Register'..." The first board of censors for this group set up shop in 1877.

For some time various methods of sorting out and defining trotting-bred horses had been furiously discussed. Also discussed was what to *call* them. In 1871, the first list of trotters that had done a mile in 2:30 or better in harness was compiled—the first "2:30 list." On it there were already five horses that had done better than 2:20—Dexter, Lady Thorn, American Girl, Goldsmith Maid and Flora Temple. Hamilton Busbey took credit for first publishing such a list. Wallace did, too. Probably so did a few other people. But this 2:30 list, whoever published it first, gave the breed a standard to shoot for (2:30 was very fast for 1871), it gave the Registry a standard to judge by, and it gave the evolving breed a name, at last—the American Standard Trotting Bred Horse. This has long since been shortened, for obvious reasons, to Standardbred. Many felt that this name wasn't grand enough, and pushed for something more elegant-sounding. But it seems to me to be perfect, for it points out clearly that here is one breed that was developed according to a standard of performance, rather than relying on beauty or bloodlines alone. Merit.

In November of 1879 a committee of the National Association of Trotting Horse Breeders presented the first official "standard" to a "large enthusiastic and harmonious meeting... and it was unanimously adopted as follows."

The Standard of Admission to the Registration

In order to define what constitutes a trotting-bred horse, and to establish a BREED of trotters on a more intelligent basis, the following rules are adopted to control admission to the records of pedigrees. When an animal meets the requirements of admission and is duly registered, it shall be accepted as a standard trotting-bred animal.

First.—Any stallion that has, himself, a record of two minutes and thirty seconds (2:30) or better; provided any of his get has a record of 2:40 or better; or provided his sire or his dam, or grandsire or granddam, is already a standard animal.

Second.—Any mare or gelding that has a record of 2:30 or better.

Third.—Any horse that is the sire of two animals with a record of 2:30 or better.

Fourth.—Any horse that is the sire of one animal with a record of 2:30 or better; provided he has either of the following qualifications:

1.—A record himself of 2:40 or better.

2.—Is the sire of two other animals with a record of 2:40 or better.

3.—Has a sire or dam, grandsire or granddam that is already a standard animal.

Fifth.—Any mare that has produced an animal with a record of 2:30 or better.

Sixth.—The progeny of a standard horse when out of a standard mare.

Seventh.—The progeny of a standard horse out of a mare by a standard horse.

Eighth.—The progeny of a standard horse when out of a mare whose dam is a standard mare.

Ninth —Any mare that has a record of 2:40 or better, and whose sire or dam, grandsire or granddam, is a standard animal.

Tenth.—A record to wagon of 2:35 or better shall be regarded as equal to a 2:30 record.

This standard of admission has been revised now and then, as time and the further development of the breed required it. In 1944, for instance, the revision by the United States Trotting Association tightened up the requirements considerably, which is to be expected as a breed establishes itself as "purebred." But it was still wide-open compared to the Thoroughbred Stud Book, say, or the Saddle Horse registry, as for example—"A mare whose sire is a registered Standard horse, provided she is the dam of two performers with Standard records."

And the loophole at the end of the list is telling—"A committee of three breeders shall be appointed to register as Standard any horse which does not qualify under the above five rules, if in their opinion he or she should be registered Standard." The biggest difference between these two versions of the Standard is in their definition of a performer.

In 1879 it was a 2:30 horse. By 1944 it was "2:20 or faster for two-year-olds and 2:15 or better for all other ages." A full fifteen-second drop in the Standard is remarkable, and certainly the fact that the trotter was bred to a speed standard is primarily responsible for this rapid improvement.

In 1882, the first volume of the Register to be published after the Standard was adopted came out. In it for the first time stallions were given registry numbers, and old Abdallah, who died on his feet in a shack on a barren beach, became "Abdallah I."

But now comes a return to the races, where all these bloodlines, crosses and families were being trotted out.

13
TWO GALLANT LADIES

It is "a cruel task," when writing a book such as this, to be forced to leave unmentioned many of the great horses of their times, and a difficult one to choose which of those many to mention. Therefore, while it is a cold way to go about it, the descriptions here will be confined to some of the horses that, by the stop-watch, were deemed the *fastest*, even though this approach automatically leaves out many superb performers. And, in this chapter, we'll concern ourselves with the record-setting trotters, the pacers deserving a section of their own.

This period, of about 1840 to about 1900, was one during which the horses, the training methods, the vehicles used, the tracks, and the races changed a great deal. For a time, there was a bewildering number of "new records"—to saddle, to wagon, "in harness" (to sulky), and at several distances, from one mile to (in 1853) Conqueror's record of 8 hours, 55 minutes and 5 seconds for one hundred miles! All this is further complicated by such categories as "time-trial" versus "in a race;" team records for pairs of trotters; three-abreast and four-in-hand records; on half-mile and mile tracks; and so forth.

One complication that aroused a great deal of debate was the method of going for a time-trial record with a sulky equipped with a wind shield or a dirt shield, and/or a pacemaker—perhaps equipped with both. The pacemaker was a harnessed running horse that preceded the trotter by a few feet or yards in order to decrease the wind resistence. This was widely disapproved of, as "trotting in a vacuum," although horses in actual races often did the same, following closely until the stretch was reached.

Then, too, we have to keep in mind that before the automatic timer was invented, there was a wide-spread affliction, according to Easterners, anyway, known variously as "Kentucky thumb" and "Indiana paralysis," the main symptom of which was the sufferer's inability to press his stop-watch until just *after* his friend's horse crossed the starting line. There was also a tendency toward "short tracks" out West (again, according to Easterners) which caused some big Eastern buyers like Robert Bonner, when traveling to see a horse go on a western track, to "carry surveyors' chains in their carpet bags."

The general public's attitude toward trotting races during this time is hard to define. It fluctuated wildly, and it fluctuated wildly by sections of the country, so that it might be extremely popular in one area at a given time and outlawed somewhere else. In general, however, most of the time it was a sport avidly pursued by all classes, and lithographs were constantly printed of the famous trotters at their work, as well as of prominent "road-riders" and their well-known "pairs." These lithographs were often paid for by harness companies and the like, which distributed them as advertisements. The extreme popularity of such prints would be hard for us to imagine now.

Trotting races were always much more popular than running races, once they got started, because trotters were still the people's horses. Thousands upon thousands of buggies, wagons, and carriages would dangerously crowd the roads to the race tracks on the day of an important "trot", and most of these vehicles "brushed" each other on the way to and from the races. There must have been countless injuries to both man and beast from the breakdowns and collisions that inevitably resulted from such insane traffic. By around 1850, trotting races often had a bad name in all but the sporting circles, from the gambling and drinking that accompanied them.

In 1849, an obviously un-sporting reporter wrote in the Cambridge Chronicle:

> On Thursday last a race came off at the 'Course' in this city, which is deserving a passing notice: It was considered a great occasion by those who take pleasure in such amusements; so we should judge, by the immense number of vehicles, some of which were crowded to excess, which passed over the road to the scene of the operation. The roads were excessively dusty, from the want of rain, and the racing on them between West Cambridge and Boston, must have been anything but agreeable. One of the horses on the Course beat anything ever before heard of—trotting his mile in two minutes and twenty-six seconds! This was rapid traveling—equal to the locomotives. And here, as we understand it, was an important point settled, and settled forever, viz.: That a horse can travel a mile in a very short space of time! Another feat performed, which should also be chronicled as a fact deserving attention, is, that more liquor was drank that afternoon, than was ever drank before, in the same space of time, in this great city. The quantity was about in proportion to the speed of the fastest horse. Now, we have come to the conclusion, that the advantages resulting from horse racing are to be found in the improvement of the breed of horses; and that the benefits accruing from fast drinking will be manifest in the improvement of the other breed!

That traditional hotbed of the trotting races, the country fair, was not always such. Not long after these agricultural get-togethers were started, in fact, editors of such prominent journals as *The American Agriculturist* were complaining bitterly about the "trials of speed" that had been introduced into these affairs, and the fact that fair-goers were spending their time watching races instead of admiring the giant sows and new inventions in farm machinery.

The fight between the "agricultural fanatics" who were trying to keep their fairs pure, and the sportsmen who wanted to trot horses, was long and at times little short of desperate. But with the emergence of such "stars" as Dexter and Flora Temple, who often appeared at fairs and thereby increased the attendance enormously, the battle was won. The emotional hold that fast trotters had on the people was just too great to be resisted. By 1860, this hold had become a national obsession, and in spite of such distractions as a Civil War, in spite of the real ordeal that travel of any kind was in those times, a trot between two beloved "queens of the turf" could attract as many as 50,000 people, including reporters and correspondents from newspapers from all over the country— and even from Europe!

This period was also, by the records at least, a mare-dominated era for the trotters. The first of these ladies to receive wide acclaim was the gray mare Lady Suffolk. Foaled in 1833 on Long Island, she was another inbred Messenger, that great horse being her grandsire on both sides. Hiram Woodruff knew "the gray lady" well, and he described her as being very little over 15 hands high, well-made, "long in the body, back a little roached," with "powerful long quarters." He also said she had a very straight neck, and "she went with her head low, and nose thrust out," which is exactly how the lithographers depicted her. For fifteen years Lady Suffolk, a dark gray who gradually turned near-white, was the undisputed queen of the trotters.

Her owner, David Bryant, would be considered a slave-driver today, and was considered so even then by the kind-hearted Hiram. From 1838, as a five-year-old, to the end of 1853, she then being twenty, Hiram tells us

> she met almost all the celebrated horses of the day, and trotted no less than one hundred and thirty-eight races, besides receiving three forfeits. As they were all races of heats, and many of them four or five heats, I estimate that she took the word from the judges above four hundred times, perhaps nearer five hundred. She won eighty-eight times... When it is remembered... that the heats in her races were as often two and three mile, and sometimes four-mile heats, it will be plain to everybody that the mare had inherited in great perfection the hardy constitution, unflinching game, and enormous stamina with which her grandsire, Messenger, was so eminently gifted. It was all but marvelous that until she was more than twenty years old the gallant gray mare stood up under the system, or rather want of system, pursued by her owner, and, in season and out of season, always answered when he called.

Fortunately, the grand old mare was finally retired, bought by a kindly man and allowed to rest peacefully until her quiet death. Unfortunately, however, although attempts were made to breed her, she never gave birth to a foal.

While she was in the midst of her long and unbelievable career, Lady Suffolk, as a twelve-year-old in 1845, became the first horse of record to cross the 2:30 line, trotting a mile in 2:29½ and beating Dutchman's 1839 record of 2:32. By 1871, twenty-six years later, when the first 2:30 list was compiled it would include 151 horses, "some of which had no right to be there," according to Busbey. Nonetheless it constituted an impressive increase.

Even before Lady Suffolk began to fade from the scene the next record-setting mare had arrived, in Flora Temple. "The bob-tailed nag" in Stephen Foster's "Camptown Races," Flora Temple would soon be even more famous than "the gallant gray lady." Two more dissimilar mares could hardly be imagined. Lady Suffolk was elegant and bloodlike, with her long, low trot, while Flora Temple was tiny (only 14.2 hands), compactly built, and had a quick, "nervous" gait. Both apparently possessed "steel and whalebone" constitutions, however.

Flora was foaled in Oneida County, New York in 1845, the year Lady Suffolk broke the 2:30 barrier. She was a bay, *perhaps* sired by a stallion named One Eyed Kentucky Hunter, and out of Madam Temple, a mare supposedly sired by "a spotted Arabian horse," whatever that might have actually been. We know a little about her early life. Busbey remarked that she was sold as a four-year-old for $13, had several owners, and even though wild and capricious, served time in a livery stable. Obviously her potential greatness was unsuspected for some time. Later on George Wilkes, editor of *The Spirit of the Times*, wrote a biography of the stub-tailed bay mare, and his account of her purchase in 1850 by a Dutchess County farmer, Jonathon Vielee, is delightful.

Mr. Vielee was standing outside his house one morning, as Wilkes told it, when a cattle drover came along the road with a little bay mare tied to the back of his wagon. He relates:

> It is not impossible, (if a certain theory of animal intelligence be true) that, as she dropped her large, intelligent eye reflectively upon Mr. Jonathon Vielee, she thought, just at the moment when Mr. Vielee mentally exclaimed, 'That's a mighty game-looking little mare!'—we say it is not impossible, that, at that very moment, she might quietly have thought, 'There's a man who knows something about a horse!'
>
> And Mr. Jonathon Vielee would not have been misrepresented by the little mare, had she ever given utterance to the idea. He had a sharp eye for the points of a horse; he had dealt a great deal in that way; and, as he gazed at the little mare's bloodlike head, traced her fine, well-set neck, firm shoulders, strong, straight back, long barrel well ribbed-up, powerful forearms, fine pasterns, short cannon bones, and general display of muscle, he thought he would like to inquire into her mouth, and take a peep or two at her feet.

Which he did, after "due civilities" with the drover, "and it struck him, that, if he could get her for any sum short of $250, she would be a mighty good bargain." He finally got around to asking her price, and, Mr. Wilkes wrote,

This inqury of Mr. Vielee's was the opening of a highly scientific display of diplomacy... which, after lasting some three-quarters of an hour, during which the little bay mare was put through all her paces in one of Mr. Vielee's wagons, resulted in her passing... into the possession of Mr. Vielee for the sum of $175.

'And a pretty good price at that,' said the drover to himself on pocketing the cash, 'for an animal that only cost me eighty and who is so foolish and flighty that she will never be able to make a square trot in her life.'

A very bad prediction, as it turned out, for two weeks later Vielee sold the mare to a New York City road-rider, George E. Perrin, for $350, and she soon learned to behave. "The crazy, flighty, half-racking and half-trotting little bay mare became a true stepper, and very luckily passed out of her confused 'rip-i-ty clip-i-ty' sort of going into a clean, even, long, low locomotive-trotting stroke."

She was soon winning match races, was given a name—just Flora at first—and was sold to Perrin's brother John for $575 that same year. Then she had an accident that made her "apprehensive, wild and flighty" again and she was laid up all during 1851. In 1852 she was back, won some more races, and in December she was sent to the best trainer of them all, Hiram Woodruff. In frigid December, mind you, and yet without special training, she was matched to go the best three out of five heats against the highly regarded horse Centreville, and beat him in the first three heats.

Hiram described Flora's gait: "Flora does not amble to begin; but, in jogging off slow, she goes rolling and tumbling along, as if she had no gait at all, and was capable of none. But when she squares away, and begins to deliver the real stroke, she has as fine and even a trot as any horse in the world." On the basis of that one race, with Centreville, Flora was sold that winter for $4,000!

During her career Flora Temple became the first 2:25 trotter in 1856, and then the first 2:20 trotter in 1859. She also raced every "celebrated" horse then racing and at one time or another beat them all more times than they beat her. She even won a match against Ethan Allen and his running mate. Her most persistent rival was the California mare, Princess, driven by James Eoff, the king of the manipulators. Flora defeated this rival several times, once even after throwing a shoe, cutting herself, and being "in a hobble all the way home."

Right after that, in 1859, the two met again, competing in two-mile heats. Flora again cut herself, and this time Princess won. Two months later there was a re-match, with Flora now healed, rested, "wild and rank." Said Hiram, "she meant mischief." All this time, by the way, Eoff had managed to make the public believe that he was holding Princess back and could win any time he chose. His reason for this: usually in a match race the proceeds from tickets were split between the drivers. The more intense a "rivalry" that could be built up, and the longer it lasted, the more people there were who would buy tickets to watch and to bet. So there was an enormous, profitable crowd on hand this day, to see Princess and Flora go one-mile heats, three in five.

In the first heat Flora, in "one of her great rushes," won in 2:23½, a full second better than had ever been trotted before. "The people were well-nigh crazy with joy," Hiram reported, although "many yet believed that Eoff could win the race if he liked to do so." But after a bad start Flora took the second heat in a boggling 2:22! And then came back to win the third in another 2:23½!

Hiram reported, "There had never been anything like such a trot before. The best previous time had been beaten by two seconds, and it had been beaten in all the heats. The rejoicing caused by that victory of hers spread from the shores of the ocean where it was achieved to the distant States and Territories... for this little mare had become a national character."

But the duel went on, exciting and profitable. In their last real race, two-mile heats, two in three, Flora won the first heat and nearly distanced Princess. The second heat had its ups and downs—first Eoff cut in on Flora, then, on a turn, "Flora ran over a man who had no business being there, and then broke"—but so did Princess. At least she broke—I don't think she also ran over the man who had no business being there. Anyway, at the end, Princess was "dead-beat and tired" and Flora won in a jog. Hiram's conclusion: "The question of superiority... had now been fairly tested. It was found that, while the California mare was second to no other but Flora, she certainly was second to her."

Upon which the two mares "went hippodroming." This was then a custom in which a famous horse or two traveled about the country doing exhibition races or time-trials. So eager was the populace to see in the flesh these favorites they'd heard so much about that a great deal of money could be made this way. Hiram Woodruff didn't approve of it any more than he approved of races in which one horse had a running-mate, but Flora had long since gone from his hands.

During this period of hippodroming in 1859 Flora, with Princess forever at her heels, made her famous mile in 2:19¾ in Kalamazoo, Michigan, setting a new world's record and becoming the world's first 2:20 horse.

Meanwhile, Flora had other challengers to contend with. The stallion George M. Patchen was one. In 1859, between beating Ethan Allen now and again, Flora was also "whumping" George M. Patchen. By 1860, he was "improved," and made another stab at it. The first race was in June, mile heats, and Flora won in 2:21, 2:24, 2:21½—a remarkable race, and Patchen was only a step or two behind her. She beat him a few more times, but when they were racing once again a most astonishing thing happened. "Just as Patchen was getting the best of it," said Hiram, "a band of men ran out at him, and threw clubs and hats in his face. In consequence, he broke..." and Flora won the heat. Patchen was then withdrawn—due to shattered nerves, perhaps, or simple fear of Flora's enthusiastic backers—and the judges named Flora winner of the race! The most astonishing thing about this disgraceful affair is that it was apparently not all that uncommon.

Flora and Patchen, and the other contenders for her crown, went at it for two more years, and eventually she simply wore all of them down. Some were faster than she on some days, but not one of them could out-last her during a long, hard campaign. Her last race was in 1861, against Ethan Allen and his running-mate again, and the team beat her the first two heats. This sort of race obviously had nothing fair about it, but even beaten, Flora was remarkable. In the last race of her life, while "Ethan and friend" beat her, they had to equal her 2:19¾ to do it, and even then they only had her by a head!

The fantastic little mare had been in 112 races over a ten-year span, and had *won* 95 of them, against the toughest competition, which, her speed records aside, makes her something very special in the way of a trotter.

In 1857 Flora's equal was foaled, another mare, who became the next "glamor horse" of her day. Her name was Goldsmith Maid, but her adoring countrymen knew her as "the Maid." Many things about this incomparable mare are worthy of note. A daughter of Alexander's Abdallah, sired by him before he left Orange County to pioneer in Kentucky, her dam is described as "an old worn-out road mare," named Ab. Since she was too wild to break to harness when young, she would be eight years old before she was raced that way, but was said to be the winner of many back road saddle races among the young scamps in her farm's vicinity. Sold in 1865 to Alden Goldsmith for $650 and a used buggy, she was then trained, with great difficulty, to wear a harness. About that same time, she came to the renowned driver, Budd Doble, and for the next eleven years, she reigned supreme on the harness tracks from coast to coast.

14

GOLDSMITH MAID AND RARUS

In some ways "the Maid" was even more remarkable than little Flora Temple. At first, after she was broken to harness, Budd Doble wrote that "she was very rough-gaited, and would only occasionally strike a square, pure trot." Perhaps she was one of the thousands of natural pacers who were "born fifty years too soon." At any rate, this was solved by Doble having her trotted slowly all spring.

And although she learned to trot and to tolerate a harness, the Maid was always a bit of an eccentric. In Budd Doble's own words,

> Of course so intelligent a mare as Goldsmith Maid and one that had been on the turf for so many years got to know a great many things... She was just as well aware when a race was coming off as was the secretary of the track. After standing quietly all day, toward late afternoon and race-time, she would become nervous, jump, kick, rear, and plunge about in the stall... Even after we would put her harness on and take her out of the stall there was no diminution in the excitement she showed. She would stand quietly enough while being hitched to the sulky, but she would shake and tremble until I have heard her feet make the same noise against the hard ground that a person's teeth will—that is, her feet actually chattered on the ground.. The instant I would get into the sulky all this would pass away and she would start in a walk for the track as sober as any old horse you ever saw.
>
> This faculty of remembering things and of actually seeming to draw conclusions for herself...was brought into full play when she went on the track to trot a race against other horses. She was always trying to get the best of her opponents and from the time we left the barn until the race was over there was never an instant that she was not figuring on some part of the race. For instance, when we would turn to score the Maid would measure the distance between herself and the other horses, would seemingly calculate the chances on getting to the wire on even terms or ahead of them, and if she concluded that they would have the best of it there was no use me trying to get her there first, because she simply would not go (forcing the judges to ring the recall bell for a fresh start)... On the contrary, if she had a good chance to beat the other horses in scoring, she would go along gradually with them until pretty close to the wire and then of her own accord come with a terrible rush of

speed so that when the word was given she would amost invariably be going the best clip of any horse in the party. Once the word was given she knew it as well as any of the drivers... If she had the pole she would make it a point to see that no horse beat her around the first turn, seeming to be perfectly aware that the animal that trotted on the outside had a good deal the worst of it, and she had no intention of losing her position next to the rail unless she was fairly out-trotted.

As to her off-track intelligence, Doble described how the Maid "was very fond of certain people" while not taking at all to others. She never really liked Doble himself, and her very favorite person was her groom "Old Charlie" who cared for her and slept in her stall all these years, and her second favorite was a little dog. Doble said, "They were a great family, that old mare, Old Charlie, and the dog, apparently interested in nothing else in the world but themselves."

I have been unable to find a written description of Goldsmith Maid, surprisingly enough, except for Busbey's brief "she was a mare of wiry frame." Her lithographs and one photograph dated in 1874, however, show her to be evidently either bay or brown with no markings, very long-legged, angular of hip, straight-necked and small-headed, with long, powerful-looking shoulders and a generally loose-coupled look about her. The photograph, in particular, very much reminds one of a modern-day Thoroughbred, especially about the head and neck. She had a distinctly neat and dainty look.

Goldsmith Maid may have been the most widely campaigned horse ever. In 1866 Budd Doble "and other parties" bought her from Alden Goldsmith for $20,000, and in 1869 they sold her for $37,000 to the partner of the financier Jay Gould, but Doble always trained and drove her. During her eleven-year career, she lowered the world's trotting record seven times, the last time when she was nineteen years old, in 1876. The next morning after this phenomenal feat, the newspapers announced it to a delighted world with the no-explanations-needed headline, "TWO FOURTEEN!" That same year the elderly queen beat the stallion champion Smuggler in a full six-heat race, every heat being trotted in under 2:20!

In all, this really incredible mare won 332 heats in 2:30 or better—by far the record in that respect, and won her owners over $206,000 in races, plus an untold amount in exhibitions. She traveled over 100,000 miles for her races and on the annual tours that attracted millions of her adoring fans. She crossed the continent three times, her last trip to California being in 1877, as a twenty-year-old.

It was that year, in California, that she met the coming-champion, Rarus, driven by another famous driver, John Splan, and a peculiar meeting it was. Mr. Splan's book, *Life with the Trotters*, tells us the story of Rarus.

Rarus was foaled in 1867, so he was a full ten years younger than the Maid. He was bred by a retired stage carpenter named R. B. Conklin, who had a little farm on Long Island, "where he began in a modest way the raising of a few colts." In a New York City market he had run across and purchased a large bay stallion that for some reason he was sure was sired by old Abdallah, Hambletonian's sire. Conklin put the stallion to work on his farm and named him Conklin's Abdallah. He also owned a well-bred mare named Nancy Awful, a descendant of Black Hawk. She was gray, and could trot in under three minutes without any special training. Conklin had enormous faith in these two. Splan said that "It was really a sort of religion with the old gentleman—this absolute belief in the greatness of the stallion and the mare owned by him, and that their union would result in a phenomenon among horses."

When a bay colt was born to them, Conklin took the best care of him. He built him his own special little stable, with an adjoining room complete with fireplace, where he would sit by the hour explaining to visitors how wonderful his colt would be some day. Many of his neighbors "really thought the old gentleman had become a little daft on the subject." Boring, too, no doubt.

But when in due course of time the bay colt had been broken and trained, he proceeded to beat such horses as the champion Smuggler and many other "good 'uns." By 1877, he was in John Splan's hands, and the curious story of that last trip to California begins.

Doble was older and much more well-known then than Splan, and he had given the younger man valuable help and advice in the shoeing and training of Rarus, as the bay colt was named. The two drivers were good friends, which is what gives the following account its peculiar flavor. Hearing that Doble and the Maid would be going to California again, and Rarus's owner being willing, Splan hitched a ride in Doble's box-car. The two fast horses then went hippodroming in the Golden State.

Remember that these were strictly exhibition "races," between the two, and Rarus was never expected to beat the two-fourteen mare. Gambling was not allowed (officially) and the advertisements made it clear that these were *just* exhibitions. The crowds were glad to pay their money just for a chance to see the fabulous Goldsmith Maid—and there was always the chance that she might break her own record and that they would then be witness to the historic event.

There appears to have been no rivalry whatever. In fact, the two drivers would work each other's horses out and so forth, and all went well until Rarus began to show such form and condition that Splan came to think that he might actually have a chance of beating the Maid, and of making some extra money for himself at the same time if he played his cards right. We'll let Splan tell it his own way, but keep in mind that he wrote all this years after the race took place, after severe criticism from the newspapers for it, and after having been "accused of everything in the world except murder in the first degree," which probably explains his noticeably defensive tone.

It all started when, just as Doble and Splan were preparing to return East,

... the proprietor of the Oakland track advertised a purse, free for all horses, entries to close at a certain day. I did not ask Budd whether he was going to trot Goldsmith Maid, and he did not ask me whether I intended to start Rarus. I did not think Budd would enter his mare, from the fact that I had heard him say that he would never start her in another purse. When the entries were opened, I was somewhat surprised to learn that Budd had nominated Goldsmith Maid. I had entered Rarus, and I think sent a check for his entrance. I saw the proprietor of the track, and he informed me there were only those two entries, but that if I would guarantee to give Goldsmith Maid a race, he would let the money go for those two. I never knew what he said to Budd, if anything; but I don't think he had any talk with him about it. I had already, in my own mind, concluded to give Goldsmith Maid a race at that time, although I did not care to state so to the proprietor of the track, as that was a matter that I thought would be worth something to me to keep to myself. Anyway, the proprietor accepted the entries, advertised the race to come off in connection with the balance of his meeting, and I commenced to get my tools ready to give people what Jack Phillips calls 'a yearly killing.' I never talked to anyone about the race in any way, shape or manner, with the exception of a gentleman of the name of Kenner, whose acquaintance I had made while in San Francisco, and who was in the habit of doing a little betting, occasionally. I worked my horse out about three days before the race, and then and there decided to back him and try to beat Goldsmith Maid. I went to Mr. Kenner, stated the case to him, told him that I was sure I could beat the Maid, pointed out that she was old, and that if it came to a long-drawn fight, Rarus must certainly wear her out, and that I believed that he could out-trot her in the first half-mile of the first heat. I further told him that if Rarus did not beat the Maid, I would be more mistaken than I had been about a race for a long time.

Mr. Conklin was in San Francisco at the time, but he never seemed to take much interest in the details of the races. He always appeared to be satisfied to leave everything to me, and never wanted to bet any money, with the exception of what I bet for him, and for that reason I never said anything to him about this race. Mr. Conklin's son was there, but I did not even tell him, and if I remember rightly, he had a few small tickets on Goldsmith Maid... I saw Budd occasionally, but I did not consider that he had any claims to know my business, and I did not tell it to him. The betting opened on the race two or three days before the day fixed for it, in the Lick House Saloon, Goldsmith Maid starting off the biggest kind of a favorite. On the day of the race Mr. Kenner played Rarus rather carefully (betting Splan's money for him, too, remember,) not daring to pile it on too hard for fear it might spoil our chances. When the day of the race came on and the people arrived at the track, they were a little surprised to see a man continually backing Rarus against Goldsmith Maid at the odds. So persistently did this man play my horse, that at the end of an hour he had forced him up in the betting considerably... A friend of Budd's came down to the stable... and told him in my presence how the betting was. Budd seemed to realize that there was something going on, and he... asked me what I thought made that betting. I told him very frankly that it was my money going on Rarus. He seemed surprised, and then I told him further that I would win, sure. At this time it was raining and continued to do so until it was likely to make the track slightly disagreeable. Budd went to the judges' stand and objected to starting the Maid, on account of the weather. The judges told him that he would have to start her, and that if he did not they would pick out some other man to drive her for him. I myself felt a little shaky, knowing that Rarus was a very poor mud horse, and I concluded that if the rain continued for any length of time, I would try and draw him, and in that way get the money declared off. When we scored for the first heat, I found that Rarus could easily out-trot the Maid. She had the pole, and I concluded to trail until she turned into the stretch. We went to the first three-quarters of the mile in that way, but as we started home from the head of the stretch, Rarus threw off a quarter-boot and made a wild break, something I had not seen him do in six months. I merely pulled him up, and made no further move for the heat, Budd winning in a jog. When we got the word in the second heat I set sail to make the Maid go from start to finish. She out-trotted Rarus around the first turn, but in going down the back stretch I got head-and-head with her, keeping very close to her. Budd called me to pull out, saying that, if the Maid made a break, she would certainly go into the fence. I did not pull out, simply kept my place, and, as we passed the half-mile pole, she made a lunge and a break, and tore off one of her quarter-boots, cutting her quarter. All this I saw at the time, as she was nearly as close to me as Rarus was. From there on, Rarus won easily, his time being 2:19,¼.

This was the first mile in a race he had ever gone better than 2:20. After the heat, Budd wanted the judges to draw the mare on account of her foot, which they declined to do, and Rarus beat her the next heats, without an effort, in 2:19,¾, 2:20. After the finish of the deciding heat a lot of people who had bet their money on Goldsmith Maid, thinking they had a sure thing, and who had gone around San Francisco all winter saying that I did not dare to beat Goldsmith Maid and that Budd had control of both horses and a contract on Rarus, I being simply driving for him, set up a howl, and said that they had been cheated out of their money, and that they would stand no such nonsense. They did not suppose to let a New Yorker come over there and trick them in that way. They asked the judges to declare the money off, and at one time it looked as though they would accomplish their object. The judges, however, after a fair investigation, concluded that the race had been trotted on its merits... This race probably shook up San Francisco as bad as anything since the last previous earthquake. Of course, there was a tremendous howl in the newspapers, and I think the reporters who wrote it up must have been the most industrious men in the world. Up to then they had always treated me fairly well, but from the time Rarus beat Goldsmith Maid until the first edition of their papers came out, they found out more mean things about me than I had been able to learn about myself in a lifetime. They seemed to think that I was the sole promoter of the 'felony,' as they were pleased to term it. A good many of Budd's friends sympathized with him, and, as they had lost their money, blamed me, for what reason I could never see, as I did not, I am sure, compel them to bet on Goldsmith Maid, and I always supposed until that time that a man had a right to bet on his own horse. Budd, naturally enough, felt very badly. To begin with, he loved Goldsmith Maid as no other man ever loved a horse, and he felt as I or any other man of sentiment would at seeing the favorite animal of his life defeated. I don't think Budd ever accused me of treating him dishonorably in the matter, in any way, shape or manner.

It may be stated here that Rarus never again met the Maid, although there were some purses offered that Mr. Doble could have started her for had he seen fit. As a matter of fact, she never started again against any horse, but, after giving a few exhibitions in the early summer of 1877, was retired from the turf, and put to breeding at the Fashion Farm of Mr. H. N. Smith, who had owned her for many years.

Afterward Rarus at Buffalo, New York, thrilled a tremendous crowd by trotting a time trial of 2:13,¼, making him temporarily the world's fastest trotter, whereupon he was purchased by Robert Bonner for $36,000 to drive on the streets of New York.

As to Goldsmith Maid, when she retired she was twenty years old. There at the stud farm in New Jersey we have our last poignant glimpse of "the golden girl of harness racing," as told by Budd Doble:

> Of course when the Maid left the turf it necessitated a dissolution of the partnership between herself and Old Charlie, who had been her companion and groom for so many years, and I am sure that both of them were very sorry when the day came. I have told how intelligent Goldsmith Maid was and how much she thought of Old Charlie. Both of these traits of her character were well illustrated two years after she had quit trotting. By this time she had by her side at the Fashion Farm a fine colt, and was very cross when anyone came near her—in fact inclined to be vicious—and as she was always a willful mare when her temper was aroused, the attendants at the farm kept a respectful distance from her. About this time Old Charlie was in the East and went down to Trenton to see the Maid and her colt. The boys at the farm told him that she was very vicious and that it was not safe to go near her, but Charlie only smiled and told them to watch him. He went to a point near where the mare stood and placing himself in a position where she could not possibly see him, he began calling her, using the name of 'Mamie,' by which she was always known in the stable.
>
> The change that came over the Maid when she heard the familiar voice was an astonishing one. She whinnied with delight and began pacing restlessly up and down to discover where Old Charlie was. When he came in sight she ran up to him and was just as pleased to meet him as one human being who had a strong affection for another would have been. She was not only not at all cross, but seemed to call his attention to her colt and when he went away the old mare stood in the paddock and looked after him with as much sorrow in her eyes as could be imagined. After he had gone a distance she seemed to think that perhaps he was going to leave her for good, and so after a moment's hesitation the old mare started out after him, leaving her colt behind, and it was only when she was caught and haltered that she would return.

There would soon be more great mares on the trotting tracks, but none of them would ever quite take the place of Goldsmith Maid.

15

MAUDE, SUNOL, NANCY, AND LOU

Rarus's reign as trotting king didn't last long. The very next year, in 1879, another gelding named St. Julien cut Rarus's 2:13¼ down to 2:12¾, but that record was also short-lived. In 1880 a quick, hot battle for the crown took place between St. Julien and a chestnut mare named Maude S.

Her origin was particularly significant in that she was the first trotting champion to have come from Kentucky, all the others having been Northern-bred horses. And, said Hervey, she was also the first champion to come from a large stud farm, rather than having been bred by some fellow who happened to own a fast road mare. She was foaled in 1874 at R. A. Alexander's Woodburn Farm, sired by Harold—a son of Hambletonian out of Miss Russell by Pilot Jr. Her grandam, Sally Russell, was a Thoroughbred daughter of the famed Thoroughbred stallion, Boston. Thus Maude S. was the first "reigning queen" to be more or less scientifically bred, and as such, a forerunner of today's "commercially produced" Standardbreds.

Maude S. was a light red chestnut in color with no markings. She was 15.2½ hands in front and 16 hands behind, and so definitely possessed the well-known trotting pitch. She was, although good-sized for her time, slender and bloodlike in appearance. At first she was mixed-gaited (that repressed pacing blood again) but with 19 ounces on each front foot she was forced to trot. Her gait, thus acquired, was long and smooth, her stride in full flight measuring a remarkable 18½ feet.

At Woodburn's 1875 yearling sale, she was sold to James Bugher for $250 and was given the unforgettable name of Sadie Bugher. At two she was broken and at four, in the hands of the Kentucky trainer W. W. Bair, she set her first record by trotting in 2:17½ at Lexington, resoundingly beating the previous world's record for that age, 2:24½. This was such a fabulous performance that she was at once purchased by one of those New York City road-riders, William Vanderbilt, for $21,000. For a time, Vanderbilt used her as a road horse, but evidently he couldn't resist finding out what his young mare could really do. In 1879 he sent her to a professional trainer on Long Island to develop her speed. She was soon returned, and pronounced to be too willful, mixed-gaited, and generally nutty to train. But when she was then sent back to Bair, he soon had her racing and winning, and even breaking Goldsmith Maid's "in-a-race" record of 2:14½ by a full second!

Meanwhile, St. Julien had done 2:12¾ the previous year, remember, in a time-trial. So in 1880, Maude S. was set to try for that record at Rochester, New York. The same day, at the same track, St. Julien was scheduled to try to beat his own time. And a most extraordinary thing happened: each horse, separately, trotted in exactly 2:11¾. Then a very brief but intense see-saw battled ensued. St. Julien did 2:11¼ at Hartford, but only three weeks later Maude S. completed a mile in 2:10¾ at Chicago. At that point St. Julien was through—he'd done all he could do—and Maude S. was Goldsmith Maid's true successor. In 1881 she lowered her own record to 2:10½, then to 2:10¼. There was absolutely nothing "in training or in sight" that could race against her after that, so for the next two years she was Vanderbilt's road mare again, although Bair was brought from Kentucky to care for her—which makes one wonder, all things considered, if he were the only person who could cope with her "nuttiness."

But then she had to come out of this early retirement, because her crown was bring seriously threatened by a trotter named Jay-Eye-See, who was also grandsired by Pilot Jr. This upstart, while Maude was resting on her laurels, had trotted in 2:10¾, a half-second away from Maude's title. So in the spring of 1884 back she went in training, being then still only ten years old. In August, Jay-Eye-See became eternally famous for being the first 2:10 trotter in history. The very next *day*, however, Maude S., accustomed to this sort of thing by now, came back with a 2:09¼. Then she "retired" again, having quickly scotched another threat.

Jay-Eye-See, by the way, was a truly historical horse, as well as an oddity. His 2:10 seemed to have knocked the stuffing out him and he disappeared, lame, only to return eight years later as a *pacer* and to become, with 2:08¾ the world's first 2:10 or better horse at both gaits!

But Maude S.'s story still had some surprises left. The first was when Vanderbilt, two weeks after her 2:09¼, sold her to his intense rival Robert Bonner. This caused a "prodigious sensation," and was never publicly explained. Although at $40,000 Vanderbilt did make a handsome profit, he certainly didn't need the money.

In any event, it was assumed that, like all Bonner's horses, Maude S. would never be trotted publicly again, but back she went to Bair, with the result that in 1885 she trotted her best mile ever, a 2:08¾, that would stand as the world's record for six years. It was also the seventh time she had lowered that standard. She was then officially retired, although Bonner had a great deal of fun with her, no doubt, in his road-races. She died at 27, still the property of Bonner's heirs, although as much as $100,000 had been offered for her.

Her affect on the public's emotions was fully equal to that of Goldsmith Maid's, Flora Temple's, or any other horse in American history. She was "venerated," and for a long time after her eleven-year reign, baby girls were named Maude in astonishing numbers.

In 1886, two more mares were foaled that would become world trotting champions. Out in California at Leland Stanford's Palo Alto farm, a bay filly named Sunol was dropped, sired by Electioneer, the stallion that Stanford had bought against all expert advice. Sunol's dam was Waxana, reputed to be a Thoroughbred, sired by Lexington himself. Sunol was put into Stanford's famous weanling track and showed great speed. But she was very nervous and her entire training process was a skittery one; she fought every step of it, and resisted domination by man in any form. Therefore she could not come out as a yearling, as so many of Electioneer's get did. When she did make it to the track, however, she made her presence felt. As a two-year-old, she lowered the record for that age to 2:18, which was remarkable in that 2:18 was also the three-year-old record at that time. Starting a year late, she was already a year ahead of herself!

Meanwhile, back in Kentucky, and just as the "Wilkes-Electioneer" feud was at its peak, a well-regarded Wilkes-bred colt named Axtell was backed as being faster than the California filly. Axtell had been bred in Iowa by C. W. Williams, a man who started with nothing but by 1885 had a small but thriving business, two mares, and high hopes. That year he sent his two mares to Kentucky with a friend, with orders to look around and see what could be done about breeding them to Wilkes-bred stallions. Most of George Wilkes' sons were too busy and too expensive, but the friend managed to book the mares to two of them. The better-bred mare, Gussie Wilkes, was "engaged" to Jay Bird, whose fee was $100, while the inferior mare, named simply Lou, was bred to another son of George Wilkes, William L., at only $50. William L. was a superb-looking horse, being related to the beautiful Mambrino Patchen, but he was young and unproven.

The result of this $150 investment, the following spring, was two fine colts named Allerton and Axtell. Three years later Axtell, Lou's and William L.'s boy, with only his owner's amateur training, would trot in 2:12 and be sold that same day to a syndicate for a record-setting $105,000! Later, when only four, Axtell would break down, while Allerton would go on to set new records and become the champion trotting stallion. This must be the most marvelous thing that had ever happened in horse breeding—one ambitious, hard-working but poor man, two cheap mares and two cheap stallions, producing, at the same time and place, the best trotting stallions of their day.

Axtell, in 1889, was Sunol's principal rival for three-year-old honors, and there were also Allerton and Nancy Hanks, all the same age. In 1891, Sunol edged ahead of her "class" with a world's record of 2:08¼. This followed Maude S.'s by six years and only shaved half a second from it. The next year, 1892, Nancy Hanks, the other mare foaled in 1886, took the crown with a startling 2:04 flat.

But two factors must be taken into account in considering Nancy Hanks' sudden leap forward. One is that both Allerton and Sunol were lame—

Nancy Hanks, foaled in 1886, was a long-reigning queen of the tracks, and a grand broodmare as well.

"hopeless cripples"—by 1892. Another is the introduction of the "bike" sulky. All records "in harness" to this date had been made with the old-fashioned, high-wheeled sulky, with the driver sitting high atop the thing in order to see over his horse's back. Sunol and Allerton went lame before they could make use of the speedier, low-wheeled vehicle. Nancy Hanks didn't, and her 2:04 was made in front of one. Nevertheless; it was the first time a trotter had beaten 2:05.

The high-wheeled sulky was used until 1892, giving the driver a bird's-eye-view of the proceedings.

A rich dark bay, 15 hands, Nancy Hanks was yet another pretty, dainty mare. Like Maude S. before her, she was mixed-gaited to start with, and like Maude S., she was beaten in only one heat in her entire career, never losing a race. But unlike all the champion mares before her, who were all pretty much failures at breeding, Nancy Hanks had eleven foals after being retired at only 7 years old. One was crippled while young; the other ten all became 2:30 performers, or producers of performers, or both. Nancy Hanks was one of the great brood mares of the breed, as well as a national favorite and a long-reigning champion of the harness tracks.

In 1892, the bicycle sulky with its much smaller, pneumatic tires was introduced by Pop Geers at Detroit. Budd Doble had been presented one by its inventor, but it looked so ridiculous he wouldn't use it. Pop (Edward) Geers decided to give it a few whirls—he'd thought of the idea himself, earlier—and was greeted with much derision by the crowd. When his horse, Honest George, appeared on the track pulling this absurd-looking thing, Geers reported, "they thought I was an advance guard of Buffalo Bill's show." But Honest George won. He did it again the following week, and, Geers said, "after this race, Mr. Doble became statisfied of the advantage of this sulky over the high wheel and commenced to use it in his races, and it was not long before they were in quite general use...."

Even in the new sulky, however, the seat was still so high—much higher than the wheels—that the driver could see over the horse's back. When, around 1900-1910, the seat was gradually lowered, wind resistance and "drag" were cut down considerably. Drivers, down so low now, had to learn to look *around* their horses, and many of them sat on their horses' tails to keep them from flapping in their faces, but records improved rapidly. Other improvements would be made from time to time, such as ball bearings in the wheels, and bent axles that allowed the horse to be hitched closer to the driver's seat until the driver was actually straddling the rear of the horse, which was no problem unless the horse was a kicker!

It's a strange thing, but even with all the improvements in the breed, the vehicles, and the tracks; even with the world trotting record edging ever downward—Alix, 2:03 ¾ in 1894; the Abbot, 2:03 ¼ in 1900; and Cresceus, 2:02 ¼ in 1901—to many, the two-minute trotter seemed an impossible dream. The figure seemed to have a mystical hold on people. Long, intense, involved articles were published in the sporting journals that *proved* it was not possible for a horse to trot that fast! Of course, the same could almost be said for 2:25, 2:20, 2:10 and 2:05 in their turns, but Two Minutes—that seemed an especially unbreachable barrier, even after a pacer had done it in 1897. But, inevitably, it was done, and it took another mare to do it.

Lou Dillon was foaled in 1898 at the Santa Rosa Farm of the Pierce Brothers in California. A dark chestnut, her sire was Sidney Dillon, by Sidney by Santa Claus by Strathmore by Hambletonian. Her dam was Lou Milton, by Milton Medium, a relatively unknown son of Happy Medium. So Lou Dillon came on both sides from lines known for "early speed and a natural trot." Strangely, as she became well-known, aspersions were cast on her as being "unfashionably bred," although her pedigree contained five crosses to Hambletonian plus strains of Mambrino Chief, Harry Clay, and some Morgan and Thoroughbred blood. At first, some aspects of her pedigree were "unknown," but the most intensive search yet was instigated and it was finally proven beyond doubt. It also proved to be the most thoroughly "trotting-bred" of any of the former champions. Even so, Lou Dillion all her life was labeled by many as poorly-bred—sheer prejudice again.

As a yearling Lou was untrainable, being too wild and spirited. The trainer George Ramage then took her over, and worked carefully with her for the next year. When finally broken to pull a cart, she wouldn't trot—just "rolled and tumbled about," as the old-timers would have said, until one day she was scared by a dog and took off at a postively flying trot that convinced Ramage

Nevele Pride and S. Dancer used a low-wheeled sulky, adapted from the one introduced (to great derision) by Pop Geers at Detroit in 1892.

his difficulties were all worthwhile. As a three-year-old, she showed great speed in fits and starts, but she was still virtually unmanageable. And at the start of her four-year-old year she was given to the famous California trainer, Millard Sanders.

Sanders had become especially well known for knowing how to handle horses like Lou Dillon, and he saved her from having to be sent straight to the brood mare barn. She almost wore out even his great patience, but by being kind and gentle he gradually won her trust and cooperation. That winter, however, she contracted pneumonia and nearly died.

But by next spring she'd recovered enough so that her owner, Mr. Pierce, asked Sanders to take her along with the other race horses on his Eastern campaign, just for the training it would give her. Too busy racing the circuit to do much with Lou, Sanders left her at Cleveland all summer and returned on free weekends to work her out. When that fall came she went a mile in 2:08 ½,and an offer of $10,000 was made for her, and Sanders began to realize what he had there.

Later, in Memphis, she went against other horses for the first time—the champion trotter Cresceus and the pacing champion Prince Alert—just for a training exercise. In it, Sanders held Lou back until the final stretch, and when he let her go she passed the two "cracks" as if they were common road-horses. This time the offer for her was $20,000, but she went home for the winter, with great hopes for the following season. Her owner died that winter, however, and all his horses were put on the block.

Lou Dillon was bought by C. K. G. Billings, one of the amateur road-riders who didn't race his horses for money, and she proceeded to become a "matinee horse." The matinee races were held in the mornings at the great meets, and in them the gentlemen drove their own horses, usually to the light, four-wheeled wagons. Because of the often intense and well-publicized rival-aries among these prominent figures, the matinees were often more popular than the professionally-driven races.

Lou was still in the charge of a professional trainer, though, in Charles Tanner. Her first time out in a matinee race, driven by Billings to wagon, she broke two records: with her 2:06 ¼ she set a new record for mares to wagon, and for five year old mares to any vehicle. She was then set to break the mare Alix's 2:03¾, which, with Tanner behind her in a sulky, she did, her 2:02¾ only a half-second off the world's record of Cresceus.

On August 24, 1903, the dainty little five-year-old mare with so little racing experience broke the unbreakable barrier—at the Readville tract that day she trotted a mile in precisely two minutes! The uproar this caused can scarcely be imagined. There were no movies or television then, but there were newspapers, photography, telegraph, and word of mouth. Lou Dillion was soon the most famous horse in the world, the foreign press being fully as

Major Delmar, the arch-rival of Lou Dillon, was raced both "in harness" (to a sulky), and, as here, "to wagon."

excited as the American. The boost she gave to the sport was sensational and came at a time when it needed it badly—the automobile having just begun to cut into its popularity.

The uproar that shortly followed, however, was less joyful. According to Hervey, some of the horsemen with large investments in stock from more "fashionable" breeding began a vicious, extended attack on this grand little mare. In her historical mile she had been preceded by a pacemaker, and the small but powerful group against her demanded that her record be disallowed. This was in spite of the fact that the pacemaker had kept as much as 20 feet ahead of her, and therefore did not act as a windbreak at all, while records were being given all the time to horses that, in actual races, followed on the heels of other horses until the last possible moment. But the driver of the pacemaker, which was of course a runner, in order to protect his face from clods thrown up by the galloping hooves, had used a muslin screen across the front of his sulky. This too, Lou Dillon's enemies pounced on, saying that this little sheet, twenty feet in advance of the trotter, meant that she was "trotting in a vacuum." Lou's subsequent career was subject to a succession of such vitriolic attacks, most of them just about as absurd.

Her most threatening rival was the bay gelding Major Delmar, owned by E. E. Smathers, Billings's keenest rival. In 1902, Billings had put up a $5,000 gold cup for an annual owner-to-drive race, the cup to be awarded to the first one to win it twice. In the inaugural running that year Smathers had won with Lord Derby, beating Billings's horse, The Monk.

So in 1903, Billings hoped to win this time with Lou Dillon. Smathers would be driving Major Delmar. The coming race was the talk of the country, involving as it did two prominent rivals and a two-minute mare. Major Delmar was also a celebrity in his own right, having done a mile at Lexington in 2:03 ¾ to wagon. But the same afternoon, Lou had trotted the same distance in 2:01 ¾, to wagon.

The cup race which came soon after these performances attracted to Memphis an enormous crowd from as far away as Europe—and Lou Dillon realized

Here is Major Delmar working out "in harness." Note that at this time the sulky had lost its high wheels but the driver still perched atop a high seat.

Billings's fondest dream by winning it for him in straight heats. But her crowning achievement came a few days later when, hitched again to a sulky with Sanders on the reins, she trotted the fastest mile the world had ever seen—1:58 ½! Then, at the same Memphis meet, she trotted a mile to *wagon* in a flat two minutes!

Now back in Sanders's hands, this continual record-breaking, with barely any rest, was taking its toll of the little bay mare who weighed only a hair over 800 pounds. But she kept at it—hard, fast work—and trained toward even more records in 1904, although by the spring of that year she was in very poor condition, too thin, and her small body spotted with sores. In spite of this, she was raced several times, doing well but possessing nothing of her old speed. And Major Delmar was in fine shape, aiming for the third annual gold cup match. So, even though that summer Lou Dillon was taken so badly that she was reported at one time to be dying, Billings ordered her got ready for the cup, so determined was he not to let Smathers win it for keeps.

In the cup race, Lou came out for it sore and lame, and after a tremendous effort in the first half-mile, she gave out and was taken back to the barn in a sorry condition, unable to finish the race. This gave Smathers possession of the cup.

Since Lou Dillon had appeared to be all right the morning of the race, and a few days afterward could do a mile in 2:01 ¼, suspicions were widespread that she had been tampered with. So persistent were the rumors that two years later an investigation was finally made, which led to a confession by a stable man, and the expulsion from the track of Smathers's head trainer. Smathers himself was held to be guiltless and ignorant of the whole thing, and got to keep the gold cup. However, and for whatever reason, soon after that race he had lost all interest and sold all his horses.

Little Lou was still kept hard at it, given over to Budd Doble now, but in 1905 she just couldn't take fast training any more, having been thoroughly burned out by her fabulous, whirlwind two years on the track. She proved to be a successful brood mare, but in 1909 she happened to be barren and was taken to Europe for a grand tour with the Billings stable, where in various capitals she was awarded many gold cups—at last—for her owner, and then was retired for good.

Lou Dillon's two-minute mile was a "magic marker" in the history of the Standardbred. But six years before that, the pacer Star Pointer had managed 1:59 ¼. It wouldn't be fair to say that this pacing performance was ignored— but why was it not received with the nationwide, worldwide acclaim that the trotting record was? In the next chapter possible answers to that intriguing question will be presented.

16
THE PACERS, AGAIN

To follow the skein of the incredibly slow return to grace of the American pacer will require going back briefly to its beginnings. The Narragansett Pacer, one will recall, was the first new American breed, developed with astonishing rapidity in the Rhode Island Colony from imported Hobbies and Galloways and perhaps some "Spanish horses" from the West Indies. But one will also recall that these earliest American pacers were the old-style pacers, which generally performed a true pace only when pressed for speed. Otherwise they ambled most pleasantly, and therefore were for about 150 years highly prized as saddle horses. Few (if any of them) were harness horses, there being few roads in their time good enough for safe, comfortable vehicular traffic. In consideration of actual gaits, in fact, these "pacers" were more closely related to the modern-day Saddle Horses than to the pacers on our race tracks. That the original pacing strains were distinct from the early trotting strains is demonstrable. Whether Wallace was right, that this pacing blood was necessary for speed at either gait, or whether Hervey was correct in considering pacing a "by-product" of trotting and more or less a blot on the breed, you may want to decide for yourself.

Another early pacing strain was the Canadian pacer, often called a Canuck. Bred principally along the St. Lawrence River, the Canadian pacer became a distinguishable type, its description much resembling that of the Morgan: small, sturdy, hairy, quite stylish, often trappy-gaited, and docile and adaptable. The original stock came from France, England, and later New York and New England. Later yet, some Morgans were probably introduced. In any case, there was so much trafficking in horseflesh throughout the entire area for so long a time that it stands to reason that all these strains influenced one another to some degree.

By the early 1800s the Narragansett was becoming scarcer, and pacers in general were already being forced westward, as harness horses (trotters) began to be useable along the coast, and trotting races began to replace the pacing races of colonial times. Along the Southern seaboard, the main interest was in saddle horses and Thoroughbreds.

113

And it was in the early 1800s that the foundation families of our modern pacers, Saddle Horses and Tennessee Walking Horses got their start. The first of the "founding fathers" was a roan, or "copper sorrel" stallion named Copperbottom, said to have come from Quebec. In 1816 he was at stud in Lexington and was used often enough that in time there were "Copperbottoms" in abundance throughout Kentucky and the neighboring states. This whole area was still close to being wilderness, and easy-gaited saddlers, which the Copperbottoms generally were, were extremely popular.

An even more influential family, which on its own and in combination with Copperbottom's, eventually made the Kentucky-Tennessee-Missouri area famous for its saddlers and pacers, was that of Tom Hal. No one knows when he was foaled, but by 1824 he'd been brought into Kentucky. He was a blue roan, breeding utterly unknown. He too was called a Canadian, although no hard evidence remains to substantiate that he was. By this time, Wallace says, any pacer of any notoriety was automatically a "Canadian." Roan, however, was not a typical color among the Canadian pacers, nor was a lot of white. The Tom Hals were noted for both these things, as well as "glass" (pale blue-and-white) eyes. Whatever his origin, Tom Hal was a pacer, and so were nearly all his get.

Various family lines sprang from these two sources, some spreading into the Saddlebred and Walker strains, but we'll follow the one most important to the Standardbred, beginning with Tom Hal's son, Bald Stockings. He was a chestnut with a widely-blazed ("bald") face and four white legs, out of a mare by a Copperbottom son, foaled in Kentucky sometime in the early 1840s. The next link in this chain was a bay horse named Kittrell's Tom Hal, sired by either the original Tom Hal or by Bald Stockings—most likely Bald Stockings. When Major Kittrell brought his bay stallion into Tennessee in 1850, this marked the beginning of a family that would soon receive widespread recognition as "the Tennessee Hals," a family from which the first champion pacers would come.

The very reason, in fact, that Tennessee would be renowned as the home of the pacing race horse was for the success of these Tennessee Hals. In a time when natural pacers were always forced to trot in harness if possible, the Tennessee Hals refused to change their ways, so strong was the pacing blood in them, partly from its having been encouraged for its benefits in the production of saddle-gaited horses. If Tennessee were going to race, then, it would have to do so at the pacing gait, "fashionable" or not, and eventually it produced such extremely fast ones that they could no longer be shut out.

The next link was Gibson's Tom Hal, a son of Kittrell's who was a roan foaled in or about 1860, in Nashville. His dam was Julie Johnson, whose blood was partly pacing and partly Thoroughbred. Gibson's Tom Hal was mated at least twice with a mare called Lizzie, and twice this union resulted in a champion pacer. The first son of Lizzie and Gibson's Tom Hal to win fame (and virtually the first pacer to do so) was a brown colt named Little Brown Jug, whose start in life was anything but promising.

Gibson's Tom Hal's owner, a Mr. Fry, had a neighbor who owned a pacing-bred mare named Lizzie, but when he tried to persuade Lizzie's owner to breed her to his stallion, the reply was that he'd rather breed her to a jackass and get a mule, because a mule colt was a sure $50 as a yearling. And that was a lot more than he could be sure of getting for a horse colt. So Mr. Fry promised that if he would breed to Tom Hal, he himself would buy the yearling colt for $50, if it were "sound and all right." But when the resulting colt was subsequently led over it was so pitifully thin it could hardly stand, and so full of lice that its mane and tail had been eaten right away. Mr. Fry, understandably, at first refused to accept this grotesquerie. But the neighbor was so desperately poor, and needed the money so badly for his family, that out of kind-heartedness Mr. Fry gave him the $50 for the worthless colt.

For a year, after being deloused, the colt was fed up and rested and came along nicely. But then Mr. Fry rented part of his farm to a man to work on shares, and sold him Little Brown Jug, now a two-year-old, for $75. The next year in this colt's life makes the story of Justin Morgan's hardships seem like a life of ease by comparison. He was broke to harness and he plowed and cultivated all summer. He also took the family wherever it had to go and, after working all day, he was ridden by the farmer's son to his sweetheart's house and left to stand outside with no food for half the night, several times a week. By fall, he was again in a pitiful condition. And once again he was rescued by Mr. Fry, who, because his tenants were so poor, paid their doctor bill of $60 and took the again-worthless colt as repayment. Once more he was fed and rested back into shape until, in the fall of 1878, as a three-year-old, he was being taken to the local colt shows, where it was discovered that he could pace very quickly!

Therefore, as a four-year-old, he was given to a trainer and very soon became, according to Pop Geers, "one of the speediest horses that had up to that time ever been seen in harness." By now he was approaching maturity, and Geers, the all-time great of harness drivers, described the gelding as follows:

His conformation was the most remarkable of any horse ever seen upon the turf. He was only about fifteen hands high, a rich brown in color, his slim neck, small ears, large, expressive eyes, and finely-molded head, clearly showed the Thoroughbred blood which he had inherited; but the most remarkable thing about him was his abnormal muscular development. His fore legs were large, flat and well-tapered, and his hind quarters were so immense as to make him look like a deformity. Many people still believe him to have been possessed of as much natural speed as any horse that ever lived.

Brown Hal, Little Brown Jug's full brother, came along in 1879, when "L.B.J." was beginning to show such promise. He didn't resemble his brother much, being long, rangey, about 15.2 hands and 1100 pounds. But he, too, was a great natural pacer. Nonetheless, at first an attempt was made to convert him to the trot, which resulted in a rate of about 2:21, with heavy weights on his forefeet. It was wisely decided at that point to let him pace, and he was soon hitting a 2:13 clip, which made him the fastest pacing stallion then going.

Then, unfortunately, Geers relates, he "stuck his foot in a fence, and was more or less lame from that time on." And Geers should know, because in 1889, he got Brown Hal to train.

The same year, lame or not, Geers put him in a free-for-all pace at Cleveland. During this one race, the pacing stallion championship changed hands twice. Brown Hal held it to begin with, with his 2:13. But in the first heat Roy Wilkes beat him in 2:12,¾, "and for a short period Roy Wilkes was the king of pacing stallions." Still gimping, Brown Hal came back to win the second heat in 2:12,½, and regained his title. Then followed an unbelievable marathon, which we'll let Geers, Brown Hal's driver, describe as he remembered it:

> That second heat, he said, seriously affected his leg, and the next heat was won by Roy Wilkes in slower time. I rushed Brown Hal for the fourth heat, and not withstanding that his lameness kept increasing, he won the heat. When the horses came out for the fifth heat, Brown Hal was so lame that he could scarcely touch the foot of his injured leg to the ground, and when we were sent away, I could barely get him to pace at all, and during the first few rods he could not pace a 2:30 gait, and before the eighth of a mile pole was reached he broke, and before I could get him settled all the horses, with Roy Wilkes in the lead, were at least a hundred yards ahead of me at the first quarter; but about this time I succeeded in getting Brown Hal on his stride, and he seemed to be inspired with a determination to win that heat, even if he had but three good legs and his courage with which to make the effort, and he seemed to fairly fly in pursuit of the leaders. I soon overtook and passed the rear horses, but Roy Wilkes still maintained his lead until near the draw gate, when I came up to him and saw that he was so tired that he was reeling and had had about enough. Brown Hal was also in about the same condition and both horses showed signs of distress. When within a few feet of the wire I took a strong hold on Brown Hal, as to steady him, then shook him up and applied the whip once or twice, to which he gamely responded and forged ahead of his rival and won the heat by a head.

This description was given by Geers in order to show what great courage this lame horse had, which it certainly did have. Five miles at top speed on a foot that he "could scarcely touch to the ground"! But what it shows about the owners and drivers of the horses in those times is another matter. Brown Hal eventually won this race, but he could never be raced again, and the next year was retired to stud in Tennessee.

Geers' book, titled *Ed. Geers' Experience with the Trotters and Pacers*, printed in 1901, also gives us other insights into the sometimes rather startling conditions of harness racing in the old days. He tells about a horse he had in training named Robert J., a very fast pacer who defeated such famous ones as John R. Gentry and Joe Patchen, from 1892 on, and made a mark of 2:01 ½,

which was the world's harness record. After the racing season of 1894 was over I concluded to ship my racing stable to California, and try the experiment of wintering in that far-away southern climate. The owner and driver of Joe Patchen were not satisfied with the results of the different meetings between Robert J. and that horse, and when they found I was to take Robert J. to California they shipped Joe Patchen there to continue the turf contests . . . In February 1895 a special race was arranged for these two horses at Fresno, California. The date set for his race happened to be in the rainy season . . . When the day of the race came it simply poured, and the mud on the track and everywhere else was ankle deep, so the race was post-poned from day to day, and the rain continued to come down in such torrents as to dampen our spirits as well as the track. Of course, we were familiar with the usual appliances used in drying tracks, but they were of no use in the face of such a deluge . . . Among the horsemen who were there were Monroe Salisbury, Andy McDowell, Tom Raymond, Jack Curry (driver of Joe Patchen), and myself. As we were confronted with unusual conditions, unusual methods must be employed . . . so we arranged for the use of 2,300 sheep owned near there, and every day the gentlemen mentioned, including myself, would gather these sheep together and drive them several times over the track, and by night the track would be in fairly good condition, but it would rain again in the night, and the next day the mud would be as deep as ever; then the sheep would be brought out again and raced over the track. We continued this process for so long a period that I became thoroughly tired of training and racing sheep. The condition of affairs gave me no peace in the day time and at night I would dream of bleating sheep, and at breakfast I imagined I could taste wool in the doughnuts, and I scarcely dared venture on the streets for fear of meeting an old ram with a wicked look on his sober countenance, as though he was looking for some one upon whom to wreak his vengeance for disturbing his peaceful flock. Finally, one evening, we agreed to have the race the next day, however muddy the track might be; and when the race was called the track resembled a mortar bed more than a race track, and every time a horse would pull one of his feet from the mud it would sound like the good-night parting of a young man and his best girl. The mud flying in all directions subjected both drivers and horses to a genuine mud bath, and made Robert J. nervous, and he broke in the last two heats, and Joe Patchen won the race."

So much for "sunny California," and so much for the Great Sheep Race of 1895. But Pop Geers had a long way to go yet in harness racing history, and his greatest champion, Hal Pointer, was yet to come.

17
THE POINTERS

As we have noted, the pacers' climb to stardom, or even to recognition as harness horses, was painfully slow. Mr. Geers, who was born in 1851 and began to train race horses in 1872, arrived on the scene just as the pacers' rise was beginning, and being based in Tennessee, where there were so many natural pacers, he was one of the first to train them extensively. His principal handicaps, at first, were that pacers were valued for their single-footing or "saddle" qualities and rarely put in harness, and that there were practically no races for pacers yet. This meant, that as Geers put it, "pacing speed was of no value; and the horse that could pace a mile in 2:10 was worth no more in the market than one that could not pace a mile in three minutes, the only element of value being his ability and value as a saddle horse."

For many years the only "racing" done by pacers was at the local horse shows, where area stallions would be shown off first at the more important saddle gaits, and then, perhaps, ridden down the road apiece at the pace—and even then, about half of them would be racking. But the pacing instinct in the Tennessee Hals and other families was terribly strong, and only needed encouragement. (Even now, this tendency sometimes creates a training problem in Saddle Horses and Tennessee Walkers.)

In 1879, the pacers' first good break came, when the "Big Four" hit the Northern race circuits. These four pacers were Blind Tom, Mattie Hunter (driven by Geers), Rowdy Boy, and Lucy. Pacers were new to the scene, very fast, and bred from stock hitherto unheard of up North. And when they emerged from "the bushes" of Tennessee, they began showing such speed that they stirred up considerable public interest—so much so that Colonel Edwards of the Cleveland track, said Geers, "proclaimed that, at least upon that track, the pacer should no longer be considered an outlaw, and from that period dates the value of the pacing horse in contests upon the different American race tracks."

We have already seen two famous early pacers, Brown Hal and Joe Patchen, and as races—and purses—began to be offered for the "sidewheelers," many more appeared very rapidly. One reason for this rapidity is, of course, that many of the so-called (and suprisingly successful) trotters had all along been natural pacers. The trotting stallion champion Smuggler, for instance, was only a trotter by virtue of *two pounds* of weight on each front foot!

By 1894, a pacer had actually become a "national favorite." He was John R. Gentry, known fondly as "the little red horse," and that year he paced to a record 2:01½. This was eight years before Lou Dillon's two-minute trotting mile, and it made it pretty clear that soon Gentry or some other pacer would do a mile in two minutes. The event was awaited with interest, but there was nothing like the anticipation for the two-minute trotter, since pacers were still very much second-class.

In 1884, Hal Pointer was foaled, sired by Gibson's Tom Hal out of Sweepstakes, in Capt. Henry Pointer's barn in Spring Hill, Tennessee. He was a saddle horse until Geers broke him to harness as a four-year-old, and Geers considered this bay gelding to be the best race horse he ever drove. As he became experienced, he learned to rate his own speed and kept a close eye on his competitors. In 1890, Geers took him North to race, where he met California's "big horse" of that year, Adonis, beating him every time they encountered one another. This, Geers said, "greatly agitated the horsemen and sporting element of California," and the next year they shipped out another white hope named Yolo Maid, an almost undefeated mare. Hal Pointer and Geers sent *her* home, too, without once having headed the bay gelding.

But, like Brown Hal, Hal Pointer had "foot trouble," and hard tracks hurt his tender hooves. So when yet another California "big one," Direct, was sent to challenge him, the outcome of the race hinged on the condition of the track. Direct won twice, both times on tracks so hard that Hal Pointer would not extend himself. But even so, in their last meeting of 1891, "he compelled Direct to pace the three fastest heats that had up to that time ever been made in harness." The next year, his feet rested, Hal Pointer beat Direct every time.

In 1894, Hal Pointer and Yolo Maid (back for another go at him) *both* became suddenly and mysteriously ill during a race, and Hal never really recovered. His best mark was 2:04½, which at the time was a world's record. When Geers wrote his book, in about 1900, Hal Pointer was still with him, as a road horse and pet. A spoiled one, at that. "If I have the carrots for him, he seems perfectly happy and will be cheerful all the rest of the day; but if I happen to forget them, he is mad and acts as ill-natured as does a smoker when deprived of his after-dinner cigar," he declared.

By this time, Geers had left Tennessee and was training at Village Farm in East Aurora just outside Buffalo, New York. There Harry Hamlin had begun to raise Standardbreds in a big way, getting about a hundred foals a year, mostly from his two stallions Mambrino King and Chimes. Mambrino King (who is also in the Saddle Horse Registry) one remembers as "the most beautiful horse in the world," and Village Farm was soon responsible for greatly improving the appearance, as well as the speed, of the harness race

Star Pointer became the first two-minute harness horse when he paced a mile in 1:59¼ in 1897.

horse. So beloved and respected did Pop Geers become during his 53-year career that "Pop Geers Day" was held in 1924 at Wheeling, West Virginia, a day that quickly turned from celebration to appalling tragedy when Geers' trotter tripped and fell, killing the seventy-two-year-old driver outright. A tragedy, yes—but after reading his book, one can't help but feel that it was a fitting end for a man who lived most of his life for horses and horse racing.

Then, in 1889, came Star Pointer, also a son of the mare Sweepstakes— which makes her and Lizzie, both the dams of two world's champions, noteworthy, in Standardbred history. Star Pointer and Hal Pointer were not quite full brothers, though, like Little Brown Jug and Brown Hal were. Star

Pointer's sire was Brown Hal, while Hal Pointer's sire was Gibson's Tom Hal, who was Brown Hal's sire and Star Pointer's grandsire. Say about three-quarters brothers!

Star Pointer and the beautiful John R. Gentry made the years of 1896 and 1897 a championship duel of the most intense kind, which stirred up even more interest in pacers. "The little red horse" being the public favorite, Star Pointer was therefore the underdog for most of this period. In 1896, especially, "John R." was on top. He won many well-publicized races that year, and came extremely close to the magic two minutes several times, his best effort being 2:00½. Since the best trotting time to that date was the bay mare Alix's 2:03¾, this made John R. Gentry the world's fastest harness horse. In that year, 1896, he also whipped the Tennessee challenger, Star Pointer, twice.

Star Pointer had had his difficulties. Although he had been trained as a two-year-old when he was three and four, in 1892 and 1893 he could not race at all because of lameness. When five, Pop Geers got him and began to work with him, but he had to go very slowly on account of this chronic unsoundness. By the end of the 1894 season, he was sound enough to win $1500 at Chicago with an effortless three heats in very fast time; but went lame again a week later and didn't race again that year. Then, as a six-year-old, Geers brought him out for six races and won them all, his best time being 2:04½.

He was then sold at auction for $5,500 and left Geers's hands, going into those of David McClary, a totally unknown and inexperienced trainer. Nevertheless, in that same summer of 1896 he was matched against the great Joe Patchen, who trounced him roundly. After a month's recovery from this debacle, he came back against two other giants, John R. Gentry and Robert J., and was again disastrously defeated, being in fact distanced. A public outcry arose, that Star Pointer should go back to Geers; but his owner stuck with McClary, and moreover sent them against John R. Gentry again only a week later, for $5,000. "The Pinter Hoss" lost again, but this time he pushed Gentry to record-setting heats. Then the two horses separated and went their own ways, both doing very well.

By 1897, therefore, it was thought that surely one of them would soon be the first two-minute harness horse, and while each had his backers, Gentry remained the popular favorite. Star Pointer, meanwhile, had been resold to James Murphy of Chicago for $15,000, but remained with McClary for training. The summer of 1897 began spottily for Star Pointer. While in July he beat Gentry, it was obvious that "the little red horse" was badly out of condition that day. Then he beat Joe Patchen twice at Cleveland, but a week later the tables were turned. And then later, Star Pointer beat Patchen again. So no certain triumph was enjoyed by any of the contenders.

But in Readville, Massachusetts on August 28, 1897, the close race for the first two-minute mile was won. Star Pointer and McClary sped to a 1:59¼ world's record, and Star Pointer was immediately in demand for public appearances all over the country.

Now Star Pointer virtually had the field to himself. Gentry and Robert J. had both been purchased by Lewis Tewkesbury, "a fast-spending, free-wheeling operator," as a road team, and Joe Patchen had begun to fade. But "The Pinter Hoss" was kept busy enough with all his lucrative exhibitions and his stud duties. In 1898 he paced seven exhibition races, wrecking track records *every time* he appeared, and three more times coming home in under two minutes!

But his owner, Mr. Murphy, couldn't stand to own him any more. He had begun to get so nervous, watching his horse go, that he couldn't take the strain any longer, and he sold him at auction for $15,000 to W. J. White of Cleveland, who had a stud farm he had optimistically named Two-Minute Farm. Obviously Star Pointer, the two-minute horse, was the stallion to head his stud. Star Pointer was supposed to have continued his exhibition racing in 1898, but by that time his bad legs were going fast, and in all fairness he should have been retired then, at the peak of his greatness.

Instead, in a grandstanding gesture, he was matched against two old rivals, John R. Gentry (whose new owner "free-wheeled" himself into bankruptcy) and Joe Patchen. And a most miserable example of greed for glory this was. Star Pointer won the first heat handily, but broke down completely in the second with Patchen winning. Then, instead of giving it up, Star Pointer's hurting forelegs were numbed and he was sent back to try again. He made a game effort, but he simply could not pace. The great horse was distanced— certainly a sad and disgraceful way to let such a horse end its public career.

When he was then retired, he received little attention as a stallion even though he was the first two-minute harness horse, having won 60 of his 79 race heats and over $50,000. This may have been partly due to bad management. But Star Pointer, Hervey said, did not age gracefully. As a young horse he had been a rangey, powerful, 16-hand animal, impressive in appearance, but as he grew older he became coarse and heavy. Then, too, there was his well-known "bad underpinning," which in spite of his race records frightened breeders away, especially since they seemed to be evident in most of the Hals.

Therefore one might say that Star Pointer's failure as a sire was almost inevitable, he having made his grand achievements in spite of, rather than because of his inherited traits, and breeders were astute enough to realize that. The Hal family, in fact, would very soon all but disappear from the tracks, primarily because of this inheritance. While its brief glory lasted, however, it did accomplish something no other family had ever done—it made pacers not only legitimate harness race horses, but popular favorites, as well. And it produced the first two-minute mile in the history of harness racing.

18

AXWORTHY AND
PETER THE GREAT

Toward the end of the 1880s, two sires came on the scene that would help restore harness racing and the breeding of harness race horses to the exalted state they had enjoyed before the Depression that began about 1893. The first of the two to be foaled, by three years, was Axworthy in 1892.

Remember Axworthy's sire, Axtell (chapter 15) was one of the great "class of 1886," a primary rival of Sunol and Nancy Hanks, and one of the two Iowa-bred horses, Allerton and Axtell. Axtell had been sold in 1889 to a syndicate for $105,000 — this, during the spectacular boom that preceded the equally spectacular crash of 1893. When the crash came, Axtell was standing at Terre Haute, Indiana, under the care of Budd Doble and being drummed up by the syndicate for all it was worth. That Axtell was a successful sire, Hervey tells us, is proved by the fact that five of his early foals, when they were only two years old, made the 2:30 list.

A. B. Darling at that time owned another good stallion, Kentucky Prince, a grandson of Mambrino Chief. He also owned, among many other mares, a special favorite of his named Old Daisy. When the financial pinch began to tighten, Darling sold much of his stock, including Kentucky Prince, but kept all his horses that had come out of Old Daisy. One of these, Young Daisy, when bred to Kentucky Prince had produced Marguerite, who then produced seven fine foals for him. One of the seven, foaled in 1892 and sired by Axtell, was named Axworthy and was left with Doble at Terre Haute for developing.

But Axworthy was one of those gangly, slow-maturing colts, and the syndicate's eagerness to get him to the track as early as possible (to further puff up Axtell's reputation) may not have been the best way to manage him. Nonetheless, he showed great early speed and as a two-year-old was raced against another one, Oakland Baron, and was pushed too hard. The Baron beat him by about a head, in a record-setting time for two-year-old stallions, but the strain on the fast-growing Axworthy told, and he could not be "trained

123

on" the rest of that year. The next season, 1895, when 3-years-old, he went to another trainer, John Young, from Kentucky. And bad luck still dogged Axworthy, in the form of a slight lameness, so that he couldn't race all summer. By fall, though, he was sound enough to go against a couple of other colts in order to give him a "mark" for his three-year-old year, and he won the race, trotting the best heat in 2:15½. Then Darling died, and all his horses were sent to auction in December, 1896, in the worst of the Depression.

Times were so bad, in fact, that Axworthy, whose sire had brought $105,-000 in the good old days, couldn't even get a bid when he was led on the block . . . until the arrival of "the King of the Sale Ring," John Shults of Brooklyn. He owned two farms and had been, over the last few years, stocking them heavily with the best he could buy. He seems to have been, from Hervey's description, quite a character, who bragged that he always bought at public auctions and that once he had decided to buy a horse he had never let anyone else get it, no matter what he had to bid.

Moreover, he had been a friend of Mr. Darling's, and when he found out that Axworthy was receiving no bids at all he declared it a disgraceful situation and bid $500 just to get things started. As it turned out, this start was also the finish, and Shults very soon owned the (nearly five-year-old) stallion Axworthy, whether he had intended to or not. Probably he. had not, because Hervey tells us that Shults already owned a plenitude of well-known stallions, and although still young, Axworthy was too lameness-prone to race any more.

But his breeding was excellent, being in fact of the same sort that had produced Maude S., and Shults, realizing that when he sold Stranger, the stallion son of Goldsmith Maid, replaced him as his premier sire with Axworthy. For some reason this struck Shults's friends as foolish in the extreme, but in a few years it was clear that he had been wise. Axworthy colts and fillies proved to be so good that when Shults ceased his breeding operations in 1906 and Axworthy was again sent to auction, this time he brought $21,000. The buyer was "Bill" Simmons, who sent the stallion to Lexington, where he remained until his death in 1917 at twenty-five years old.

This tall, light chestnut stallion, possessed of a "slashing" trot and impressive conformation, sired many fine horses, almost none of which resembled him in the least — except in being extremely fast. The two of his sons that have brought his line through to present days were both small and bay — beautiful little horses—named Guy Axworthy and Dillon Axworthy. Their names are to be found in the pedigrees of many of the greats of the trotting horse breed.

But the "greatest of the great," in terms of breeding influence, was Peter the Great, foaled in 1895. His sire was Pilot Medium, a son of Happy Medium by Hambletonian, out of a mare by Pilot Jr. In the late 1800s, Pilot Medium, a good-looking gray two-year-old, was bought for about $120 by Walter Clark, from Michigan. The reason the price was so low was not only the hard times, but also the fact that the gray colt had as a yearling had a hip knocked down and was a cripple.

Pilot Medium was not well-received by Michigan breeders, but Clark collected a small band of brood mares, none of them of the Standard, and proceeded to breed them. His very first crop contained a gray gelding, Jack, who went on to win more money than any trotter before him. And, like his sire, Happy Medium, all of Pilot Medium's get were easy to train, early speed trotters. This had a rather two-sided effect on the big, beautiful gray stallion's stud career and reputation. On one hand, it brought him plenty of mares, but on the other hand (and coupled with his poor location) these mares were usually under-bred and their owners interested only in getting colts that could win money fast. They owned no large stud farms and had no interest in

Santos, the dam of Peter the Great, and W. P. Engleman, who was the promoter of the old Kalamazoo, Mich., track and was at one time a vice-president of The Grand Circuit.

"improving the breed" beyond that one colt or filly. Most of Pilot Medium's sons, therefore, according to Hervey, were gelded, and none of his daughters found their way into the big, successful breeding establishments, even though 127 of them made the 2:30 list!

Once again one finds the big breeders too interested in fashionableness to know a good thing when it came along. In fact, if it hadn't been for one very remarkable son of his, Pilot Medium's blood would probably not have survived, let alone come to be almost completely dominant. That son was, of course, Peter the Great.

Peter the Great's dam was called Santos, and in spite of tremendous efforts to research it half of her pedigree remains cloudy. Her sire was Grand Sentinel, a descendant of Volunteer by Hambletonian, but her female side has never been proved. Apparently it "came out of Tennessee," and therefore was quite likely to have consisted of the good saddle stock so prevalent there, but that's just a guess. She had several owners, her last being D. D. Streeter, of Michigan.

Peter the Great was not named, as one might suppose, after the Russian Czar, but after a well-known local trainer, Peter V. Johnston, who worked for Streeter. Peter the Great was an unusual Pilot Medium colt in that he was hard to train, and then seemed slow and unwilling to trot squarely. His early career was, as a matter of fact, a very close thing, all the way around. As a two-year-old, he had a "sick spell," and consequently he had to be practically re-trained. He was also confronted by an exceptionally good crop of two-year-olds that year (1897).

After struggling mightily with his colt all summer, "Peter V.," as he was called, took an enormous chance by starting him for the very first time in no less a race than the Kentucky Futurity, against seasoned opponents. He didn't win, but he was second in both heats, beaten only by the two-year-old "star," Janie T., and he trotted the mile in 2:17 ¼. This was a grand accomplishment by Peter the Great's trainer, who had had to overcome so much to achieve it.

But after wintering, he found he had to begin all over again, and the following three-year-old season was a copy of the previous one—a long period of struggling, followed by just managing to get the big colt going again in time for the Kentucky Futurity without any other racing experience. It was, in other words, only the second race of his life. And this time he really astounded everyone by winning it, and, moreover, winning it in sensational style. Trotting with head high, and in an imperious manner, he easily led the way in the first two heats of the three-in-five heat race. In the third heat, Peter V. finally let him out, and he won by fully twenty lengths, setting a new record for that race of 2:12,½ and garnering for his hard-put trainer a well deserved accolade.

That winter the remarkable colt was sold for $20,000 to J. Malcolm Forbes of Boston, who had established an enormous breeding establishment. This proved to be unfortunate for Peter the Great. Forbes seems to have been rather odd, to say the least. He was a man of great wealth, and evidently of equal vanity. He also apparently wanted to get every penny's worth out of his investments. Peter the Great was immediately put to stud service, and when that season was over, put right into training for racing again. His new trainer, a young man of "the new school," used entirely different methods but he had even more trouble than Peter V. had suffered. Tremendous weights had to be used to keep the 4-year-old trotting at all, and this, along with constant fast work, kept him more or less lame most of the time. Even so, he put in many fast, exciting races that year, some of which caused some controversy, mostly in the form of criticism of the young trainer.

The upshot was that at season's end Peter the Great's reputation had been damaged, due entirely to too much fast work on top of a season at stud. There was an attempt to train him up again in 1901, but his legs couldn't take it.

Peter Volo was a son of Peter the Great, and the sire of Volomite.

After having been in only seven races in all, but having been worked as hard for them as any horse had ever been worked, he was retired.

Forbes, who had bought many famous horses and later driven them in the local speedway races, now intended to do the same with Peter the Great. But the horse let him down badly, being ill-mannered and completely unable to cope with that kind of road-racing (which got pretty wild at times) and after several embarrassing attempts, Hervey reported, Forbes got out of the wagon purple with rage and told the groom, "Take that horse away and never bring him to me again."

So much did he detest this horse, that he had Peter the Great stabled apart from the other stallions, where he was treated very badly, and he refused even to look at him. So while the other stallions were fat and glossy and pampered Peter the Great, in his shed, grew thin and rough-coated and it was said, bad-tempered and dangerous. He was, nonetheless, occasionally used as a stud, but usually to mares too closely related to the other stallions for them to be used. One hates to think what might have finally become of Peter the Great under these circumstances, had not a Michigan-bred foal of his named Sadie Mac become the undefeated three-year-old champion of 1903.

Naturally, the gossips wondered what Forbes would do, then, as Peter the Great's condition in life was well known. It was generally supposed that Forbes would "see the light" and at least bring the stallion back to the main barn. But this odd man then did the oddest thing yet — he sent Peter the Great, who had just become famous again, to auction. Not only that, he wrote up a grand description of his breeding potential for the sale catalog, which raised eyebrows right and left among those who knew how he hated the horse. The peculiar situation also promoted much caution among potential buyers — why was Forbes in such a hurry to sell Peter the Great, no matter how he felt about him personally, when his stud career now seemed slated for such success?

There was a small crowd at the sale, and he received a generally unenthusiastic reception when the stallion entered the sale ring. He had been fattened up a little for the sale, but his legs looked very bad, especially his rear ones. One hock was huge. The auctioneer's blandishments went unanswered, until finally Peter the Great was sold to Peter Duryea of New York for $5,000, for his Patchen Wilkes Farm in Lexington.

After a brief squabble with his partner, and some thought given to sending Peter the Great to England to Duryea's other farm there, the stallion eventually arrived in Lexington to join the stallions at Patchen Wilkes Farm, with a stud fee of $100. Again the eyebrows shot up. He looked terrible, with his crooked hind legs and enlarged hock. But here he received fine care, and soon he looked much better. This, and the fact that he had trotted faster than any other stallion then available in that state soon brought him the fifteen outside mares he was allotted, he being principally saved for the farm's own mares that first season. He remained at Patchen Wilkes Farm until he was twenty-one years old, when (a good indication of his success) he was sold at that advanced age for $50,000. He lived until 1923, dying at the age of twenty-eight.

Peter Scott models some of the pads, guards, and bandages now used widely to protect the harness race horse from injuries.

During his stud career he sired more foals than even Hambletonian's 1331, although exact figures are not available. Mares were sent to him in droves from all over the country for many years, and the relatively new artificial insemination process was used extensively, which meant that he could service an almost unlimited number. By the end of his career, his fee had risen to $1,000, and still mare owners lined up.

His achievements were unparalleled in horse history. Hervey estimated that the many sons of Peter the Great sired, in their turns, at least *5,000* 2:30 horses. He himself sired an incredible 498 trotters in that list, plus 163 pacers! And many, many of them possessed record-breaking speed. Add to this the fact that he was also a great brood mare sire, and his incomparable impact on the breed is easily understood. By 1946, Hervey reported, there were 131 two-minute performers of record. Of these, 74 descended from Peter the Great. And subsequent "premier stallions" of their times were of his blood, most notable among them being Peter Volo and Peter Scott, and Peter Volo's son, Volomite.

Not since Hambletonian himself had there been such a Standardbred sire, and there may never be again.

19
"THE ROARING GRAND"

In England, Thoroughbred racing received its biggest boost from the fact that the royalty loved it ("the sport of kings"). In America, trotting races became even more popular whenever the incumbent President was a fan. George Washington is known to have owned and raced Narragansett Pacers, his favorite breed, although he bet (and often lost heavily) on the runners, too. Andrew Jackson was strictly a running horse man. But the 18th President of the United States, Ulysses Grant, who presided from 1869 to 1877, was a great trotting horse fancier. One of the most widely distributed lithographs of the time was one titled "Taking the Reins" that depicts Dexter being driven by President Grant. His enthusiasm for a fast-trotting horse was not the *only* reason for trotting's popularity at that time — but it helped, and in 1871 the Grand Circuit was first formed, with Grant's blessings.

From about 1800 to 1850, during which time trotting races gradually changed from under saddle to in harness, and pacing races were rare, there were basically two categories: the "big" races, between and among the "cracks," which took place primarily on and near Long Island and Boston; and the country-fair sort of racing, in the interior. Speed, according to writers of the period, had become a mania among city-dwellers and farmers alike. It was no longer enough for a horse to be steady and durable, it had to be fast and stylish as well. A man wrote in 1857, "Pleasure driving has become a national amusement . . . for which a growing passion is to be noted among all classes of our citizens."

As people in general became more prosperous and enjoyed more leisure time, the sport of racing harness horses — whether on an oval track or on the road to town — burgeoned apace. There were all sorts of driving horses and even more of a variety of vehicles, just as there are so many kinds of cars today. Trappy, stylish, docile little Morgans were considered ideal "family horses (not fast, but pretty) and safe for women to drive. Great, long-strided "slashing" trotters were for the more adventuresome and speed-crazy drivers. And as this period progressed, the homely, heavy wagon became supplement-

131

ed by light spring-wagons, many of them two-seaters, built primarily for speed . . . the approximate equivalent of today's sports car.

Even the two-wheeled sulky, with room only for the driver, was soon seen upon the roads as well as on the race tracks, the approximate equivalent of a street dragster! The choice of equippage was nearly limitless, and more and more of the daily traffic became definitely of the sporty variety, rather than utilitarian. If lithographs from this period are at all indicative, the traffic was not only congested, but highly dangerous, with all of these speeders on the roads and streets. One such lithograph, entitled "Going to the Trot," shows one of a team of horses with its front feet in the back seat of the wagon in front of it, a wheel falling off, the second driver shaking his fist at the first, and everyone involved hanging on for dear life. Meanwhile, a trotter and sulky are fast approaching all this mayhem from the rear, promising even more excitement to come. This increasing demand for speed naturally focused a great deal of intense attention on the formal races, and on the breeding of "the trotting-bred horse" that such races fostered. A new type, like the Hambletonians, was watched as avidly as a brand new model from Detroit is now, and if it proved to be fast it immediately became popular and many more were bred. The time-honored "improvement of the breed" justification for horse racing really meant something to the general public in the case of the light-harness horse.

A big change in the situation came about when the railroads began to spread throughout the country, from about 1850 onward. They made it possible for inlanders actually to see some of these famous horses, mostly, at first, by way of hippodroming and exhibition races. Race horses no longer had to trudge afoot from Boston to New York to Philadelphia. They could be loaded onto a horse-car and, by the 1870s, sent as far as California, like Goldsmith Maid was three times in that decade. (Race horses had been sent coast to coast before the railroads, but it was a grueling trip, whether overland or by sea.) So the railroads, while gradually destroying some of the strictly utilitarian values of the horse by replacing stage coaches and long-haul wagon teams, at the same time greatly extended and intensified the value of a *fast* horse by easily bringing high-class trotters to tracks like Buffalo and Cleveland and Chicago, and by making it much more practical to send a mare to a high-class stallion hundreds of miles away.

Thus it was that the Grand Circuit became possible and in fact, from the standpoint of organizing things, almost necessary. As a means of seeing that the best horses were all at the same track at the same time, therefore providing the most exciting races possible, it was ingenious. Prominent members of the "trotting clubs" in four different cities first got together to discuss this in 1871, continued making plans through 1872, and in 1873 in Cleveland, the inaugural race of this carefully plotted series was trotted. At first there were only the four cities involved — Cleveland, Ohio; Buffalo, New York; Utica, New York; and Springfield, Massachusetts — and the rather unwieldy name of the organization was the Quadrilateral Trotting Combination. The circuit kept expanding, however, until at one time or another it had taken in 60 different cities, including some in Canada, and its races now offer over $4 million in purses.

"Grand Circuit Week" is still the most thrilling part of any local race meet, when the biggest purses are offered for the biggest races and the "biggest horses" arrive to compete for them, even though the "Roaring Grand" is now over a hundred years old. It began, the U.S.T.A.'s "Hoofbeats" magazine recalls, before baseball had anything like a professional league, and before basketball was even invented. It longevity becomes even more remarkable when it is considered that during the century of its history, in spite of setbacks like the arrival of the automobile, "hard times," and growing competition from all the other, newer sports and amusements, the Roaring Grand is healthier now than it ever has been.

There are several reasons for this. Such "hypos" as night racing and parimutuel betting have undoubtedly been instrumental. But one big reason has been the introduction over the years of classic races, the "triple crowns" of harness racing that never fail to draw big crowds and considerable interest.

The Triple Crown of Pacing consists of The Little Brown Jug, started in 1946 and named in honor of that early pacer; the William H. Cane Futurity at Yonkers; and the Messenger Stake at Roosevelt Raceway. All give huge purses now, and of course the prestige of a win is incalculable.

The oldest of the classics is part of the Triple Crown of Trotters, the Kentucky Futurity, the climax event of the season for the country's best three year old trotters, held each fall in Lexington. It has now been held for over eighty years. The other two "jewels" in the trotting crown are the Yonkers Futurity and the Hambletonian, the most famous of them all.

The first Hambletonian Stake was held in 1926 at the New York State Fair at Syracuse. From 1930 through 1956, the Goshen track in Orange County was host. But since 1957 the Hambletonian has been trotted every summer at DuQuoin, Illinois, a few miles from St. Louis. This is *the* harness race of the year, where the very best three-year-olds compete for over $100,000. It is held during Grand Circuit Week of a meet that includes an enormous country fair, and "a good time is had by all." The Hambletonian is the closest thing to a good, old-fashioned trotting race that we have left today. The stature of this race is probably best indicated by the fact that millions of people who could not name one other horse race can name three: the Grand National steeple-chase in England, the Kentucky Derby, and the Hambletonian.

Over the years harness racing had seen many other changes, of course. The bicycle sulky that followed the bicycling craze, and that Pop Geers was brave

"Scoring for the word" in the most famous harness race of them all, the Hambletonian, at DuQuoin, Ill.

enough to try, was apparently at least partly responsible for lowering the trotting record by about four seconds. A "kite-shaped" track was in brief vogue, and horses did do better time on it, but it soon lost favor. Its odd shape provided longer stretches and fewer turns, but it also took the race too far away from the spectators in the grandstand for too much of the time. (Records made on kite tracks are followed by the letter "k".) We have seen some of the trouble caused by other innovations, like the wind and dirt shields and the use of pacemakers in time-trials, and the running-mate hitch made most famous by Ethan Allen, but all of these were relatively short-lived fads, unlike the bike sulky which has continued to be used and improved upon to this day.

Track surfaces were also much improved during the last century, from rutted, sometimes stony surfaces, to softer, better-tended ones. The mile tracks gradually gave way to half-milers, for the most part, as the growing numbers of fans demanded to be closer to the action and as surburban land values shot up. This cut down the time records a bit, and increased the dangers on the tighter turns, but, even though the half-mile track was not greeted enthusiastically by the drivers, it stayed. Few races are now run on mile tracks, or in a series of heats, although some of the classics represent exceptions. Most harness races now are mile dashes on half-mile tracks, and most are for pacers.

Another thing that made harness racing more acceptable to spectators, especially bettors, was the use of various tests to insure that horses haven't been tampered with — a far cry from the old days, when a track veterinarian might be called upon to furnish a driver with "a bottle of hop" to pep up a sluggish horse. (Some vets had invented especially good recipes for "hop," that could make a usually mediocre old mare win her race "with her ears set forward, looking for a bigger town!")

All of these changes were well under way by the end of the 1800s, although yet to come were the giant "harness racing plants" that came to life at night under hundreds of floodlights, with parking lots larger than the tracks themselves.

But the most important change was the Grand Circuit, accompanied by nationwide organization and regulation. It was during Grand Circuit Week that the folks out in the hinterlands got to see horses like Lou Dillon, Dan Patch, Greyhound, and Billy Direct, the "stars" of this new era of a fast-growing sport.

20
A NEW CENTURY

Lou Dillon ushered in the new century with her two-minute mile in 1903. Her rival, Major Delmar, also crossed that historic line in the same year. Both horses' records are tarnished by the controversy over dirt shields and pace-makers. Cresceus, a powerfully built chestnut stallion, also trotted in under two minutes in 1903, but *his* record was questioned because of possible inaccuracies in the timing.

The confusion over what was a legitimate record and what was not reached its height with the pacer that was soon the most famous, most beloved harness horse of all time — Dan Patch. He was the world's fastest harness horse, as well, for the incredible span of 35 years, his world's record standing for all that time.

Dan Patch's sire was the great black pacing rival of Star Pointer, Joe Patchen. While "Beautiful Joe" never quite managed to win the championship crown, he nevertheless beat Star Pointer and John R. Gentry, who did. And in the remarkable year of 1903, his son avenged him by taking Star Pointer's title away from him.

Dan Patch's dam was a lame mare, cheaply bought but well-bred, named Zelica. Her son was foaled in Indiana and was owned by Dan Messner, Jr. He was a mahogany bay — handsome, bright, and easy-going, and for once one can relate a genuinely happy story about a great horse. In all his life Dan Patch had but three owners, and all treated him royally. His career, although somewhat "tarnished" by the above-mentioned confusion, was a long and smashingly successful one. Dan Patch is now remembered as some sort of a "show horse" that trotted only exhibition miles. As one can readily judge, this is not true at all, and is an insult to a truly great race horse.

Dan Patch's first two years of life were spoiled, lazy ones, he was more of a pet than some dogs are. He wasn't given any training, but simply allowed to play about and to grow into a big, strapping, handsome colt. In the spring of his third year, 1899, he was broke to harness and worked gently and easily by an elderly trainer. When he turned four, he hit the race tracks for the first time — and he in no uncertain way let the world know that he had come to win. By 1901 he was ready for the Grand Circuit, and he was also sold that year to Mr. M. E. Sturgis of New York and Buffalo for $20,000. Myron McHenry, a well-known driver, took over the reins.

Dan Patch, the pacing superhero of the first decade of the twentieth century, retired undefeated and his record of 1:55¼ stood unbroken for 35 years.

1901 was the year that it became crystal clear to everyone that Dan Patch was a superhorse, one of those horses that is born ahead of his time. He won all twelve of his races that year made a mark of 2:03¾. In 1902, as a six-year-old, it took only three races for him to run out of competition. In many ways Dan Patch resembled the Thoroughbred superhorse that would follow him, Man o' War. He not only beat horses, he did it with *ease*, never extending himself at all but leaving his would-be competitors on the verge of collapse. He also, like Man o' War, loved a crowd and its adulation, and the tumult and excitement of race day. Where the two hero-horses differed greatly was in temperament. Dan Patch had none of Man o' War's arrogance and wildness, he was always cheerful and he went about his work efficiently and quietly.

By the middle of 1902 there was not another pacer in the country that cared to match its "foot" with Dan Patch, and he then became an exhibition horse. But by that time he had raced, and raced fairly hard — 56 heats in all. He had lost two of those heats, but never a race. He was undefeated and had yet truly to show his speed. And so he challenged the clock. In his very first time-trial he matched Star Pointer's world pacing record of 1:59¼! But this was only the start of an amazing series.

At this point he was sold, for the last time, to M. W. Savage, owner of the International Stock Food Company of Minneapolis. Savage was a character who more than matched his new "star," purchased for $60,000. He's also a bit hard to describe — flamboyant, boastful, an "operator" — he was all that and more. And he absolutely adored Dan Patch, as did, by now, the entire country. But Savage made *sure* they loved him.

I have on my wall right now an old print, advertising the International Stock Food Company, and Dan Patch. Thousands upon thousands of these were sent to feed and general stores, to be handed out to customers. And "Patch" was soon off on a promotional campaign that would make today's rock stars envious. He had a white sulky. He had a huge white box car, emblazoned with his name, and he had a staff to serve him. When he arrived in town (or even passed through) that day was "Dan Patch Day," and thousands gathered and waited for hours just to catch a glimpse of him. Wherever he stopped, he had to be guarded carefuly or he would have been bald soon from all the souvenir seekers after a hair from the great Dan Patch! If all the horseshoes that were sold as having once been worn by Dan Patch had really been his, he'd have had to be reshod all around about every five minutes of his life. He was one of the first "star athletes" to endorse products, and his name appeared on everything from toys and throw rugs to shaving mugs. But his schedule was heavy, and he had to work so hard for all this glory that, at the end of 1903, his driver McHenry had an argument with Savage about it and quit. Not before, however, he had driven the horse to fifteen exhibitions all over the country, and to seven different miles in under two minutes, his best in 1:56¼.

Then Harry Hersey became his driver, and the hot pace continued in 1904. With two pacemakers, one in front and one alongside for encouragement, Dan Patch set out to break his last year's record. With the other two drivers bellowing to "stir him up," he did just that, coming along in an astounding 1:56!

Meanwhile, in the springtimes, Dan Patch was also promoted as a sire, along with the stock feed. In 1905 he served no fewer than 56 mares before going back into harness to get ready for the summer's campaign, being ready by September. In the next two months, "Patch" rode his white box car 6,000 miles, put on fourteen exhibitions, and set five world's records. An offer of $180,000 was refused by the proud-as-punch Savage. And, by the end of 1905, he already had six "performers" on the standard list.

But then the confusion began in earnest. Several of his records started squabbles; sometimes he had used a pacemaker, and sometimes not. His greatest achievement, a mile in exactly 1:55, was not officially recognized because he made it with a pacemaker and a dirt shield, just after that way of going had been ruled out. His next best time of 1:55¼ *was* recognized, however, and it was not beaten until Billy Direct's 1:55 thirty-five years later. By the end of 1905, the ruling out of the pacemaker at least settled some of the confusion. And when it is considered that Billy Direct had the advantage of all those years of improvements in tracks and equipment, the pacemaker and dirt shield seem more than compensated for. The fact is that Dan Patch was the fastest pacer going at the turn of the century and that even now seventy-odd years later, he could doubtless still hold his own in any company.

Dan Patch's pace continued until 1909. He was still sound, as he had always been, but he had been going hard for nine years and Savage didn't want to risk his health. By then he had paced 73 miles at an *average* speed of just under two minutes, many of them much faster than that. He made a few more tours afterward to let his fans see him, and then was completely retired in 1913 to live a life of utter luxury.

Dan Patch died on July 11, 1916, of a heart condition. M. W. Savage died on July 12, 1916, from the same cause.

Dan Patch's line has not survived, even though he sired 38 trotters and 138 pacers in the 2:30 list, including 21 pacers that could do 2:10 or better. For some reason, the line just did not "breed on" much further.

Dan Patch did not wear hobbles, but by the turn of the century many pacers were beginning to. Curiously, this method of hanging looped straps around a horse's upper legs in an effort to keep it on its gait was first invented for trotters, in the 1880s. At that time there was still a preference for trotters over pacers, and many of those "mixed-gaited" and naturally pacing horses were being converted to the more respectable, more profitable, gait. An Indianan thought of hobbles first — being meant for trotters, they crossed diagonally under the horse's body. In the 1890s, these "Indiana pants" were being used quite extensively, but they were extremely awkward and uncomfortable, and kept breaking, and were soon given up. At that point, and as pacers were again coming to the fore, someone thought to "hang hobbles" on a pacer. This didn't require crossing underneath, the pacer being laterally gaited, so naturally it worked much better and the idea caught on swiftly.

Hobbles do not *force* a horse to pace, but they do make any other gait very difficult and uncomfortable, and they therefore cut down training time and

Uhlan, a 1:58 trotter, was the first to lower Lou Dillon's record, in 1912.

effort a great deal. Thus came about a strange reversal — instead of using hobbles, weights, and rails laid on the ground to convert pacing-bred horses to the trot, trotting-bred horses, as well as natural pacers, were being put in hobbles to help them *pace*. And as training fees and other expenses became more and more of a factor, this relatively quick and easy method became even more popular, until only a few purists remained to disdain it. One can perceive a bit later on what a profound and revolutionary impact the "hobble pacer" has had on harness racing.

In the meantime, as the new century got under way, the marathon heat races lost favor, and different systems of classifying races were tried (to thwart "manipulators" and make races fair for all classes of horses), and the sport came of age. The Depression of the 1890s finally gave way to a recovery, until 1908 saw harness racing's first $50,000 race, the American Trotting Derby. The first two decades of the 1900s in fact saw a gradual revival of interest in harness racing, but it was rather slow, principally because of the "new toy," the automobile. Horses like Dan Patch, that claimed the public's affections, probably saved the day, during these trying times.

Dan Patch was the brightest star of the first decade, but in 1912 the trotting gelding Uhlan lowered Lou Dillon's record to 1:58 flat and became enormously popular. In 1922 an even more popular trotter, Peter Manning, turned in a 1:56¾ mile at Lexington's fast track. It remained for the 30s, however, to produce the most famous trotting champion of the century, and the pacer that would, at last, lower Dan Patch's long-lived record of 1:55¼.

21

GREYHOUND AND BILLY DIRECT

Greyhound, "the gray ghost," was a superhorse in all but one respect—he never became a sire. He was foaled in 1932 during the worst of the next big Depression, and with the market again at a low point and no market to speak of at all for stallions, he was gelded. He was Kentucky-bred, both his sire, Guy Abbey, and his dam, Elizabeth, being owned in that state. His breeding was superb. Guy Abbey's sire was the great Guy Axworthy, and Elizabeth was a full sister to Peter the Brewer, who was one of the fastest sons of Peter the Great. Elizabeth was a beautiful gray mare never raced.

Greyhound, named for his color and for his racey conformation, was sold as a yearling to E. J. Baker of Illinois for $900. Baker had for years owned some of the best harness horses, including several champions, and he at once turned the promising-looking colt over to his trainer, S. F. Palin.

Greyhound, being large and "growthy" as a two-year-old, lost his first race, but as the season went on he began to catch up to his long legs and finished the year with six wins in a row.

By that time the (over-16-hand) gelding had won everyone's close attention. Like his dam, he was a beautiful horse, and with his high-headed, flying trot, the stride of which measured as much as 21 feet, he was a gorgeous sight, giving the impression, Hervey remarked, of being "invincible"—which, as it turned out, was just what he was.

As a three-year-old, Greyhound was undefeated in his eight races, the second heat of the Hambletonian being his most spectacular performance of the year. He started out well behind the strung-out field, on a break, then settled into his breathtaking trot that relentlessly overhauled all the rest, and brought him home a full 25 lengths ahead! His 2:02¼ in that race was the world's champion record for three-year-old geldings but it only stood for three days. At that time, Greyhound himself lowered it to 2:00 flat.

As a four-year-old, Greyhound met his first and only defeat, on the half-mile track at Goshen. The sharp turns and short stretches were not to the

142

advantage of such a large, long-strided horse. Even this one defeat, however, was not a total one, as he won the fastest of the heats in that race. That year, 1936, his record was 1:57¼, and it seemed certain that Greyhound would be the trotter to lower Peter Manning's 1:56¾ of fourteen years before. There was just no stopping the great gray ghost.

Greyhound's world trotting record of 1:55¼ stood for 31 years, as Dan Patch's 1:55¼ pacing record stood for 35 years. Truly two "long-reigning kings!"

The next year the suspense kept building, as Greyhound first equalled Peter Manning's record in September at Lexington, without bettering it. A year later, in 1938, he tried again, and he then became the world's champion trotter, with 1:55¼, a title he was to hold for 31 years, until 1969.

But Greyhound was far from satisfied with that, and he went on to conquer new worlds in his following seasons. As a seven-year-old, with no competition, he settled down to lowering every record anyone could think of. In August 1939, he was hitched double with Rosalind, the current "trotting queen," and together they set a new pair record of 1:58¼. Still looking for something to beat, that same year Greyhound aimed his flying trot at Peter

Guy Abbey was the sire of "the Grey Ghost," Greyhound.

Manning's two-mile mark of 4:10¼, and lowered it handily to 4:06, going at the remarkably steady rate of exactly 2:03 for each mile. It seemed there was nothing Greyhound could not do better than any other trotter had ever done before.

At only eight-years-old, in 1940, he was too young, too sound, and too popular to retire yet. So Baker entered him in seven races, and he won them all, losing only one heat. He had by then won nearly $40,000 (a great deal, considering the low purses during those depressed times) and his owner then felt that he had done more than enough to earn a glorious retirement. But what to do for a "grand finale?" Was there yet another world's record for Greyhound to smash?

It turned out there was. No one had gone for the world's trotting record under saddle since Helen James had ridden Hollyrood Boris a mile in 2:05 ¼. So it was decided that Greyhound, in a farewell appearance at Lexington, the site of so many of his triumphs, would be trotted for the saddle record. And the well-known Saddlebred show horse rider, Frances Dodge Johnson, was asked to ride him in this historic event. This she agreed to do, although she had never attempted such a thing before, and knew Greyhound only as one of his countless fans.

In retrospect, it was a risky undertaking, but, as always, the big gray horse didn't let his friends down. With the competent Mrs. Johnson on his back, in front of an enormous crowd of well-wishers, "the gallant gray" demolished his fifteenth world's record, coming to the wire in 2:01¾!

After that final, very dramatic, record-breaking performance, Greyhound led a life of ease, leaving his comfortable stall and paddock only for occasional "personal appearances" at various trotting meets. There his stately elegance, combined with his great fame and the fact that he could still produce effortless, astonishing bursts of speed, served to keep him in the public eye for many years, while his record of 1:55¼ retained for him the trotting crown for thirty-one years.

Greyhound and Rosalind ("the trotting queen") set a pair record in 1939 of 1:58¼.

The pacer Billy Direct would also during this decade set a record that would then stand for a long time—22 years. He was foaled in 1934 in Tennessee, sired by Napoleon Direct, a pacer that had given Pop Geers his first two-minute ride in the course of a brilliant career. His dam, Gay Forbes, was owned by H. H. Ridge of Haverhill, Massachusetts, and had been sent down to Tennessee where she was bred for several years to Napoleon Direct.

Billy Direct looked so fine as a two-year-old that early in the year he was bought by Nathan Smith of Massachusetts for $2,000 and given to William Carney for training. This first year he was entered in two races, and he won both of them so easily that his trainer entertained high hopes indeed. When he went to the barn for the winter, several "speed merchants," Hervey said, had their eyes on him. Two of them, P. J. Downey and D. J. McConville, bought him in January 1937 and sent him to Vic Fleming at Syracuse for training.

Greyhound's historic "farewell appearance" at Lexington in 1940, trotting to a 2:01¾ "under saddle" record, under the capable guidance of Frances Dodge Johnson.

Direct, one of the "grand old men" of the Standardbred.

Billy Direct had won his two races in hobbles, but Fleming could see that they were unnecessary, and from then on Billy was a free-legged pacer. As a three-year-old, he won all of his races again, and again all so effortlessly that great things were foreseen for him. That fall he was let out for the first time, and paced a mile heat in 1:58, which equalled Directum's race record of 1915. (Dan Patch's 1:55¼ was a time-trial record.) Even then, Billy Direct was "coasting" under the wire.

His four-year-old season, in 1938, was to prove that his trainers had not over-estimated his potential. After three wins, he lost a race at Springfield apparently because he was not "up to snuff" that day, and then easily won three more races. Then the big free-for-all pace at Lexington came up, and a ridiculous thing happened in the first heat. The horses had scored and were coming along for the start when evidently someone got excited, because the word was given to go ahead at the same time that someone else rang the recall

Billy Direct's time-trial record of 1:55 finally broke Dan Patch's record, and it in turn stood for an amazing 22 years.

bell. Of the four drivers involved, two interpreted this one way and two another, with the result that Billy Direct and another horse were pulled up, while the remaining pair paced on around the track. Obviously the whole thing should have been called a blunder and the race started over again. But instead the judges decided that Billy Direct and the other stopped horse had been distanced!

Fleming was fit to be tied about this undeserved blot on Billy Direct's record, and he asked permission to do a time-trial. When this request was granted, he brought the colt back and, to the great joy of the indignant crowd, avenged himself and then some by doing something that had for years been considered to be impossible: "going in the open," he actually shattered Dan Patch's 1:55¼ that had been made behind a pacemaker. His time that day was a fantastic 1:55 flat.

This made Billy Direct the holder of the world's pacing record, both "in a race" *and* in a time-trial, and on both mile and half-mile tracks—this combination being a record in itself. He finished out the year in "personal appearances," which added considerably to the pitiful, Depression-days $12,000 he'd won in races.

Napoleon Direct gave Pop Geers his first two-minute ride, and went on to sire the great Billy Direct.

After standing at stud for a while in Ohio, he was eventually purchased by the famous Hanover Farm in Pennsylvania, where he proved to be fully as valuable as a sire as he had been successful as a pacer. For a little fellow— only 15.2—this dark bay or brown stallion made his mark in both worlds, and his stud career would no doubt have been much more brilliant than it was had it not been cut short. Billy Direct died in 1947, at only thirteen-years-old. As it was, his line was important but soon overshadowed by others, such as the "super-sire" Volomite.

Volomite was foaled in 1926, a son of Peter Volo by Peter the Great. Another small one at 15.2 hands, and also a very dark shade of bay or brown, the trotter Volomite had a hugely successful racing career from 1928 to about 1930. But it is as a sire that he is most famous. From the very first crop onward, his foals were fabulous. The Volomites soon took over the race tracks, both as trotters and as pacers. His stud fee quickly rose to $1,000, and his yearlings brought as much as $37,000—a particularly spectacular figure in a time when prices in general were low, 1944, the end of a Depression and the start of "wartime." But the high price tags on his children were more than justified.

The famous Hanover Shoe Farm, which has been the home of many champion harness horses.

By 1946, Volomite had sired 306 Standard performers. He was the first sire ever to beget 100 sons and daughters that could trot or pace in under two minutes, and moreover, he sired 100 2:10 pacers *and* 100 2:10 trotters, an astounding record.

The only other modern-day Standardbred sire even to approach Volomite's success would arrive in 1940. Called "the greatest stallion of any racing breed," and "The Big Daddy of Harness Racing," he was the bay stallion Adios.

22
ADIOS

The year 1940 was the beginning of a decade that would see harness racing, the popularity of which had slumped badly again during the Depression of the 20s and 30s, begin its spectacular rise to its present-day status of a major American sport. Several things had conspired to throw harness racing into one of its declines.

The automobile had driven horses off the roads, streets, and "speedways" and had captured the rapt attention of the public. This meant that harness racing had lost its vital link with everyday life that had so long sustained it. In addition, during the 20s and 30s, harness racing was administered by three different associations, all claiming to be national in scope but being in reality somewhat sectional, which inevitably led to some competitiveness among them. The spectators/bettors at the tracks were also becoming increasingly impatient and disgusted by one of the sport's worst drawbacks—repeated and often interminable "scoring for the word." Drivers jockeyed for positions and tried to beat each other to the line, causing recall after recall, until it wasn't unusual for a half-hour or more to pass before the tired and nervous horses even got properly started. And, perhaps the worst drawback of all, from the bettors' viewpoint, were all those trotters breaking gait and losing any money bet on them. Then, too, there was the latest Depression.

But in the decade of the 40s, things began to look up considerably. In fact, harness racing was revolutionized entirely. Competitive sectionalism was removed when in 1938 the United States Trotting Association was formed, the first truly national organization of the sport. By 1940 it had things well in hand.

Also, in 1940, Roosevelt Raceway was opened near New York City and introduced the first successful night-time harness racing. Night-time racing was not entirely new, because the old three- and four-mile heat races had sometimes been forced to finish up in the dark. Hiram Woodruff mentioned a driver who, in the first half of the 1880s, "was killed at Chicago driving in a heat after dark." But this time they used lights! That, too, had been tried

Roosevelt Raceway, near New York City, is where two vital innovations were introduced: nighttime racing, and the mechanical starting gate.

before, as early as 1888 (with gas lights), but it had never really taken hold anywhere. Horsemen were sure that this bizarre method of racing wouldn't work, that horses wouldn't go well under such "unnatural" conditions—even though in the few cases where the experiment was tried the horses actually made three or four seconds' better time than they did on hot, sultry afternoons.

Roosevelt Raceway, a brand-new harness track then, salvaged from an auto-racing track, nearly failed in this "under the lights" experiment, too. At first the horsemen for the most part refused to have anything to do with it. Then came the war, with its black-outs in case of enemy bombers, and the races had to be moved farther away from the city for the duration. But the operators of the track persisted, and after losing money the first two years, began to produce a profit. By the end of the 40s, the track could boast a betting handle of over $68 million dollars for its lengthy, 105-night session. And New Yorkers wanted even more. The next track to string lights was

Steve Phillips displays a picture of his "machine," the mobile starting gate, that he perfected in 1940.

nearby Yonkers, in 1950, and night racing was well established as the only way to trot.

Then, in 1946, Steve Phillips made harness racing much more enjoyable for everyone concerned by perfecting a mobile starting gate that eliminated the tedious, protracted scoring. The mobile starting gate had been tried before, too, but Phillips's "machine" was the first one to receive wide acceptance. Framework wings, attached to the rear of a small truck and extending the width of the track, kept all the horses at the same speed and very effectively prevented anyone from darting ahead at the next-to-the-last second. The machine's driver merely steered, while the official starter, facing the rear, controlled the accelerator and kept an eye on the action. This brought recalls to a minimum, helped greatly in preventing accidents caused by excessive "jockeying," and meant that races could get started about when they were supposed to. Introduced at Roosevelt Raceway, the mobile starting gate had a great deal to do with improving racing and boosting its popularity. (Parimutuel betting was also introduced in 1940, in New York State, and this too was a big assist, as it made betting simpler and unquestionably honest.)

A field of pacers score behind an updated version of Mr. Phillips's gate.

Still, many bettors were put off and often enraged when "their" horses broke gait and threw their money away. This was especially true of trotters. For some time pacers, their hobbles all but preventing them from breaking, had been favorites with the bettors for that very reason, and by 1940 they were so popular that trotters and trotting races were considered by track operators to be a losing proposition. The bettors were saving their money for the more predictable pacers.

And so once again the lowly pacer came to glory. This time his dominance had nothing to do with his "easy saddle gaits" or with the lack of decent roads. It was simply that, through the use of Indiana pants, he could be expected by his backers to hold his gait throughout a whole race. Moreover, he also became immensely popular with trainers, owners, and breeders, because as a rule the training of a hobble pacer required much less time, effort, and investment. Therefore, fairly soon he could be on the track earning money, instead of jogging endlessly around the work track and eating his head off.

Adios was "the greatest progenitor the Standardbred horse has seen since Peter the Great." As a pacer, he is also perhaps the horse most responsible for the current popularity of that gait. With him is his friend and driver, Frank Ervin.

This emergence of the pacer as a dominant strain in the Standardbred was enhanced by the apparent fact that while trotting-bred horses sometimes produce pacing get, pacing-bred horses seldom sire or give birth to trotters. Also, throughout the long, early period when trotters reigned supreme and pacers were unprofitable (there were no races for them, and, as Mr. Bonner had announced, "No gentlemen drives a pacer") many natural pacers had been forced to trot. This situation no longer existing, and pacing actually being encouraged, all those natural pacers were now *allowed* to pace—just as soon and as fast as possible.

Delvin Miller's faith in Adios as a potential sire was proved to be well-placed when Adios became the biggest sire of money winners of all time, Standardbred or Thoroughbred.

Thus it was that "the world was ready" that January 3, 1940 when a foal was born to Hal Dale and Adioo Volo on Two Gaits Farm at Carmel, Indiana... a foal that was to become the greatest progenitor the Standardbred horse had seen since Peter the Great. And that foal, a little bay colt soon to be named Adios, was a pacer.

A quick look at Adios's pedigree explains it all. It contains no fewer than 35 crosses to Hambletonian, through eleven of that founder's sons, including George Wilkes, Happy Medium, and Electioneer. The Mambrinos and the Clays are also represented. Most important, however, is the fact that all of this fine trotting blood was combined in Adios with that of the famous Tennessee Hals, those early pacing stars, through his sire Hal Dale. So while this pedigree is not surprising, it does represent one of those rare, supremely fortunate genetic combinations that result in a true "phenomenon." For Adios was just that, and—unlike Blue Bull, for instance—he appeared on the scene at just the right time.

Hal Dale (2:02¼) was a pacer by performance and by blood. He was sired by Abbedale, by The Abbé, by Chimes, by Electioneer, the stallion that Leland Stanford took to California. He was born, raised, and died in Indiana, a state that for many years was considered the center of Standardbred breeding, with many fine stud farms within its borders. Hal Dale was foaled in 1926 and lived until 1955. His dam was also a pacing-bred pacer, Margaret Hal. Foaled in 1914, she was sired by Argot Hal, a double-gaited performer, who was in turn sired by the great Brown Hal.

Adios's dam, Adioo Volo, was sired by Adioo Guy (2:00¾), who descended from the only son of Hambletonian that paced, Strathmore. Adioo Guy's grandsire, Sidney Dillon, was the sire of Lou Dillon. Adioo Guy was extremely inbred, his sire Guy Dillon being bred to a full sister of his own dam. Adioo Guy was used at stud for several years in America before being exported to New Zealand in 1929. And just before he set sail, he sired Adioo Volo.

Adios, the end product of all this crossing and inbreeding, was sold by Two Gaits Farm as a yearling at the 1941 Indianapolis Speed Sale, bringing the highest price of any of the yearlings there, $2,000. His new owner was Thomas Thomas of Cleveland, and his trainer was Rupert Parker. Adios was taken to Parker's winter quarters in South Carolina to be educated, where a peculiarity of his developed. The infield of the training track was used for barns, and near the finish line there was almost a "path" across the track to the infield gate, made by horses and carts heading for the barns. When Parker saw that his pupil, Adios, tended to spook and leap over these tracks, he tried to eliminate this habit by slowing up as he approached them. This trick worked, as the colt calmed right down and quit his jumping. It didn't occur to Parker at that time that when they approached the "path," they were also approaching the finish line.

Whether this was the reason, no one who cannot read a horse's mind could say for sure, but in his first race at Old Orchard Beach, Maine, in 1942, Adios gave Parker a rather nasty surprise. Not in the first heat, however. In that one, the 15-hand bay colt shot past a field of ten other "babies" with apparent ease to win in 2:02½, a half-second off a ten-year-old world's record for that age-group. Therefore it was even more of a shock when in the second heat Adios was battling it out in the stretch with King's Counsel. King's Counsel edged past him, Parker went to his whip, and Adios dropped to a walk!

This would happen again, more than once, in the next two years. Parker naturally thought this horrible habit had something to do with that early training "trick," and of course he tried everything he could think of to correct it. Nonetheless, while Adios was obviously a speed demon, and set many records, every once in a while he unexpectedly threw on his emergency brake at the last moment.

In early 1944 Parker was taken gravely ill and he chose Frank Ervin to take his place. Before their first race together, Parker advised Ervin not to push Adios too hard, as he was by that time convinced that that was where the problem lay. Following this advice, Adios and Ervin took second place. Then Parker died and Ervin was on his own, and subsequently he made his own discoveries about Adios. He found out that, far from not wanting to be pushed, the colt resented being held back, and therefore did his best when let out the whole way. He also discovered that Adios's sulking was at least partly due to the whip, and from that time on he never used it on him, merely "changing the bit around in his mouth" to distract him and keep him on his toes.

Adios was racing during wartime. Purses were small, and there weren't many really high-class contenders for them, so during the winter of 1945 Adios was sold. His buyer was Harry Warner of Warner Brothers movie fame, and a partner. They paid $15,500 for the stallion, an exceptionally good price considering the times, and Ervin and Adios went West.

It was to be a low spot in Adios's career. Although he did set the world's record out there for pacing on a 7/8-mile track, he had more bad luck than good. Once he even collided with the new-fangled starting gate. Warner appears to have been difficult to work for, and at the end of that first year, 1945, he and Ervin came to a parting of the ways. Shortly afterward, Adios went lame at only six years old. Warner evidently decided he might as well use the stallion one way or another, and he established a breeding farm rather suddenly, buying some brood mares from Indiana.

Adios's first crop of foals—only five of them—appeared in 1948 and at that point Warner and his partner rather suddenly decided *not* to have a breeding farm, after all. They sent everything in the barn to the Lexington sale that fall.

Although he had broken seven world's records in his career, and was probably the fastest pacer in America, Adios had only won $33,329, a figure wholly due to the wartime doldrums. Breeders understood this all too well, however, and there were several of them who wanted to own this stallion. Adios's luck returned in full measure when Delvin Miller got him for a bid of $21,000. Miller was a great horseman, a famous and hugely successful trainer-driver, and a highly respected member of the harness fraternity. Adios couldn't have fallen into better hands when he was taken to Miller's beautiful Pennsylvania home, Meadow Lands Farm.

The sum was a great deal of money then, and Miller—along with a lot of other people—held their breath to see what sort of colts and fillies Adios would help produce. As is often the case with unproved sires, but especially in hard times, his first couple of batches were out of less than the best mares. In spite of that, in a few years Adios pacers were sweeping all before them and setting new records right and left. Adios died in 1965, and by 1968 his sons and daughters had won over $17 million dollars, which makes his record-setting stud fee of $12,500 understandable. Up to 1967 he had put 365 yearlings in the sale rings and their average sale price was a whopping $18,512. His final crop of yearlings in 1967, consisting of ten colts and fillies, brought a total of $429,000! All of these figures are impressive. In fact, they make Adios the biggest sire of money-winners of all time, Standard-bred or Thoroughbred. But while this is an indicator of a sire's value, it is also an indicator of the state of the economy and the state of harness racing during a given period.

An even better indicator of a sire's greatness is "Time." A horse that can do a mile in two minutes or better is a darned good horse, whether it cost $200 or $20,000. And Adios sired 78 two-minute or better pacers, among them three world's champions that could do 1:55 or better! He also sired the dams of 77 more two-minute pacers. His grandchildren, and now his great-grandchildren, dominate the racing scene so completely that it has become hard to find a list of "today's winners" that does not include some of them.

Small wonder, then, that Adios is revered by many as the greatest progenitor since Hambletonian himself, and a major force in making harness racing the spectacularly popular sport that it is today.

23
AFTER ADIOS

So many record-breaking horses were sired by Adios that it's hard to choose among them "the best" of the lot. The fastest, however, at least by official record, were Adios Harry, Adios Butler, and Bret Hanover, all stallions.

The first of the three to arrive was Adios Harry, in 1951, bred by L. T. Hempt of Harrisburg, Pa. Purchased for only $4,200 as a yearling, this brown horse turned out eight miles in two minutes or better and earned a record $345,433 during his career. His best mile of 1:55 was a new record, eclipsing two unofficial records—Billy Direct's 1:55 in 1938, which was a time-trial record, and Dan Patch's 1:55, was not officially acceptable because of the runner in front of him. This pacer also set a new two-heat record (1:55 2/5—1:56 1/5) and a new record for the one and a half mile distance. In 1956 he even set a world's record in the *mud*, 2:07 1/5 at a mile and a sixteenth. After his great racing career, Adios Harry sired two, two-minute or better performers and 67 who could turn in a time of 2:05 or faster.

Adios Butler came along in 1956, and his potential was enhanced by the fact that his dam's sire was Billy Direct. He was bred by R. C. Carpenter of Chester, N.Y. and sold as a yearling for $6,000. A bay stallion, Butler set so many new records that his four-year career seems to consist of little else. Twenty times he beat two minutes, on all kinds of tracks, with and without hobbles. He was the first horse to win pacing's Triple Crown, in 1959, and in 1960 he beat the time-trial record of his grandsire, Billy Direct, in a trial of his own in just 1:54 3/5. There was no other reasonable choice for Horse of the Year in 1960 and 1961, after he was purchased by a syndicate for $600,000. He was ceremoniously retired at the end of 1961, and went on to be a credit to his line in the stud.

The bay colt foaled in 1962 named Bret Hanover, however, was the greatest of all these great children of Adios, in the opinion of many. He first saw the light of day at Hanover Shoe Farm in Hanover, Pa., and was bought for $50,000 as a yearling by Richard Downing of Cleveland. His trainer and driver was none other than Frank Ervin, and together they ushered in a period that has been called the Age of Bret.

161

In his first season on the track, as a two-year-old, Bret showed the stuff he was made of by becoming the first horse of that age ever to be elected Horse of the Year, in 1964. And again we are confronted with an almost numbing array of records. He paced the fastest miles of that year on mile and half-mile tracks, won all of the two year old pacing classics, and was, of course, Two-Year-Old Pacer of the Year. He also won more money than any other two-year-old ever had before, $173,298.

Adios Harry set several records "apace," including the in-a-race record of 1:55. One great race horse, he went on to sire many others.

1965 saw little change in this remarkable march through the records. That year he racked up ten world's records, nine stake records and six track records, and brought his total earnings, in just two years to $515,082. This constituted another record, and he also won 35 consecutive heats, yet another record. Thirteen more times that year he paced faster than 2:00, and, now a three-year-old, he scooped up the Triple Crown as he flashed by. Again, he was Harness Horse of the Year.

In 1966, he continued his high-speed string of victories, records and titles. Among other things on his busy agenda was a match race at Yonkers that was billed as The Pace of the Century. His opponent was the gamest little gelding this side of Seabiscuit, a ten-year-old named Cardigan Bay.

Adios Butler, by Adios out of a daughter of Billy Direct, was the first horse to win pacing's Triple Crown, and the horse that beat Billy Direct's time-trial record of 1:55, after the record went untouched for 22 years, by going 1:54 3/5 in 1960.

The horse that Bret Hanover was sent to meet that day at Yonkers has been described by one writer as "an orthopedic case." When a six-year-old in New Zealand, Cardigan Bay had suffered a really terrible accident. While he was being jogged, a cart wheel had fallen off and spooked him so badly that he had dashed away to his barn, the collapsed cart careening behind him. After the inevitable crash when horse and cart met the barn wall, Cardigan Bay's right hip showed gleaming white bone through a hideous wound. Ordinarily, a horse so injured would have been put down, but such was his racing record that he was saved, slung up to redistribute his weight, and treated for pain.

Bret Hanover, driven here by Frank Ervin, was the most famous harness horse of modern times. Horse of the Year from 1964 to 1966, and a Triple Crown winner, he set many records and became one of the breed's most successful sires.

Courageous Cardigan Bay, with one hip six inches lower than the other, and other infirmities, beat the great Bret Hanover in 1966 in "the Pace of the Century."

After four months of this ordeal, he was out of his stall again but he could scarcely hobble, and one hip was six inches higher than the other! Nonetheless, he was trained once more.

It seemed impossible, but, crooked or not, two years later Cardigan Bay was the most famous pacer in New Zealand and Australia, and that year (1964) he won the Inter-Dominions race. He was also that year purchased by an American syndicate for $100,000, on the advice of the famous driver-trainer, Stanley Dancer.

In 1965 "Cardy" was a surgical case again, having a small, fractured bone removed from his leg. In spite of these and other physical handicaps, like bad ligaments, Cardigan Bay in 1968 became the first harness horse ever to win a million dollars.

So it was this plucky little horse that met Bret Hanover in 1966 in the Pace of the Century. In front of 36,000 spectators, Cardigan Bay beat the Horse of the Year, in two minutes flat. (Later, in a "revenge match," Bret Hanover won.)

But Bret Hanover was a big, hardy horse—calm and always in good shape. After his unexpected defeat by Cardigan Bay he went to Lexington, where so many records have been made and broken on the famous "Big Red Mile" and set the greatest record of his three-year career. It was October 7, 1969 (Frank Ervin drove him as usual), and he aroused the huge crowd to a screaming frenzy when he paced under the wire in a first-time-ever speed of 1:53, 3/5.

While this was his fastest mile, a time-trial, a few days later he ran perhaps his most significant one. It was his last win in a race, and in it he paced 1:59, which brought him to a really phenomenal *thirty-one* two-minute miles, finally beating Dan Patch's 50-year-old record of thirty! This race also gave him $922,616 in "lifetime" (three years) earnings. In an "arrangement" that involved $2 million, Bret Hanover then went to the famous Castleton Farms at Lexington, where he proved to be probably the most successful of all the successful stallions sired by Adios, his very first crop of yearlings selling at an average price of $21,850 in 1969. Like nearly everything else about these fantastic Adios horses, this average was a record.

The last ten or twenty years in the history of the "American Standard Trotting-Bred Horse" have seen such an upsurge in the breeding and training of them that there has been a comparable multitude of "stars." The prices given for promising colts and fillies, and the purses to be won by them, have climbed into the stratosphere until "figures" today are similar to those of the Thoroughbred industry. Today's harness racing scene is a far cry from Hiram Woodruff's time and the days of "fast road mares." The harness racing fan, although avid as ever, is more apt to be someone who knows very little about horses *as* horses. He may be well-versed in statistics and very competent at handicapping, but he has probably never met a horse face-to-face, let alone enjoyed a wild brush down the road with his neighbor's new filly.

Fresh Yankee, a trotter, was the first North American bred harness horse to win over one million dollars. His driver here is J. O'Brien.

Albatross, a pacer driven here by S. Dancer, was one of the few modern-day harness horses whose names became familiar to the general public.

Albatross and Nansimond, two "good uns," battle it out for the lead.

And, perhaps most symbolic of all the changes, a record-setting performance is now reported not on the front page of a newspaper (as Goldsmith Maid's "TWO FOURTEEN!" was) but back in the sports section. Once in a while a harness horse comes along whose name is recognized outside "the harness fraternity"—the trotter Fresh Yankee, the first North American bred harness horse to win over $1 million, and the brilliant pacer Albatross come to mind—but most modern "cracks" come and go with relative swiftness and are soon replaced from the crowd of other speedsters. Harness racing today is big business. Even the drivers, who now often fly their planes from track to track and earn fabulous sums of money in a successful year, are businessmen. To try to describe such a scene would mean soon being lost in a morass of statistics.

But even now there are countless people in this country who still keep one or two brood mares, every spring taking them to the best stallion they can afford—and every one of them has high hopes and a chance of realizing them. For despite all the big breeding establishments with their several "divisions," every so often one of these small breeders comes up with a real winner. And maybe some day—out of some small pasture, perhaps, or out of a big band of

Waiting for the bell.

high-priced mares—there will emerge another harness horse so sensational that it will become another "national favorite" like Dan Patch or Flora Temple. The odds are unimaginable against it. There are probably too many other sports and amusements nowadays for a harness horse to attract that much attention and affection from more than the racing fans themselves.

But there have been superhorses before who did the impossible. There could be one again. There even could be, some day in the future, a pacer or a trotter of such heroic proportions that one morning the *front* pages will shout, "ONE FIFTY!"

Bibliography

Ainslie, T. *Ainslie's Complete Guide to Harness Racing*. New York: Trident Press, 1970.

Busbey, H. *The Trotting and the Pacing Horse in America*. New York: Macmillan, 1904.

Geers, E. F. *Ed. Geers' Experience with the Trotters and Pacers*. Buffalo, N.Y.: Mathews-Northrup, 1901.

Goodall, D. M. *Horses of the World*. New York: Macmillan, 1965.

Herbert, H. W. *Frank Forester's Horses and Horsemanship of the United States and British Provinces of North America*. New York: Stringer and Townsend, 1857. Two volumes.

Hervey, J. *The American Trotter*. New York: Coward McCann, 1947.

Hill, M. *Adios: The Big Daddy of Harness Racing*. Cranbury, N.J.: A. S. Barnes, 1971.

"Hoofbeats." Official publication of the United States Trotting Association. Vol. 39, No. 3, May, 1971.

Mellin, J. *The Morgan Horse*. Brattleboro, Vt.: The Stephen Greene Press, 1961.

Pines, P. A. *The Complete Book of Harness Racing*. New York: Grosset and Dunlap, 1970.

Splan, J. *Life with the Trotters*. Chicago: H. T. White, editor and publisher, 1889.

Stong, P. *Horses and Americans*. Garden City, N.Y.: Garden City Publishing Co., 1939.

Sullivan, G. *Harness Racing*. New York: Fleet, 1964.

"Susanne" (E. E. Scharf). *Famous Saddle Horses*. Louisville: The Standard Printing Co., 1942. Volumes I and II.

Wallace, J. H. *The Horse of America*. New York, by the author, 1897.

Welsh, P. C. *Track & Road: The American Trotting Horse*. Washington: The Smithsonian, 1968.

Wolverton, C. C. *Fifty Years with Harness Horses*. Harrisburg, Pa.: Stackpole, 1957.

Woodruff, H. *The Trotting Horse of America: How to Train and Drive Him, with Reminiscences of the Trotting Turf*. New York: J. B. Ford. Boston: H. A. Brown, 1869.

Index